Self-Confidence

Self-Confidence

A PHILOSOPHY

Charles Pépin

Translated from the French by Willard Wood

WITHDRAWN

OTHER PRESS / NEW YORK

Production editor: Yvonne E. Cárdenas
Text designer: Jennifer Daddio / Bookmark Design & Media Inc.
This book was set in Goudy and Wade Sans by
Alpha Design & Composition of Pittsfield, NH

1 3 5 7 9 10 8 6 4 2

Library of Congress Cataloging-in-Publication Data

Names: Pépin, Charles, author.
Title: Self-confidence : a philosophy / Charles Pépin ; translated
from the French by Willard Wood.
Other titles: Confiance en soi. English
Description: New York : Other Press, 2019. | Includes index.
Identifiers: LCCN 2019017402 | ISBN 9781590510933 (hardcover) |
ISBN 9781590510940 (e-book)
Subjects: LCSH: Self-confidence.
Classification: LCC BF575.S39 P4613 2019 | DDC 158.1—dc23
LC record available at https://lccn.loc.gov/2019017402

For Victoria, Marcel, and Georgia

Because I only have to look at you to feel confidence.
In myself. In life. And most of all in you.

Contents

Self-Confidence

Introduction

The training wheels came off this morning. All of four years old, she hops on her bike and takes off under a blue sky. Her father runs alongside, one hand at her back, the other gripping the bicycle seat. She pedals faster and faster, clutching the handlebars. Her father encourages her: "Don't stop pedaling," he says. "Look straight ahead, you're doing great!" He lets go of the seat. The child picks up speed. She maintains her balance, rolling along without her father's help. When she realizes it, she shouts with joy and speeds ahead. She feels buoyant and free: she has confidence.

But what does she have confidence in, exactly?

In her own abilities? In her father? In this moment of family happiness?

Self-confidence, we sense, is the result of alchemy. It arises from a combination of factors. The paths leading us to it are various, but once we achieve self-confidence, it works the same for each of us. There is only one self-confidence, but there are a number of ways to get there.

Madonna is a stage animal, an artist who has been able to reinvent herself all her life. Yet she was a shy child, scarred by the loss of her mother when she was only five. So how did she find the strength to make her mark?

Patrick Edlinger was one of the pioneers of free climbing. When he free-soloed a route, his gestures were so fluid that he seemed to dance above the void. He moved from one handhold to the next with extraordinary grace. What was his secret?

Landing on an aircraft carrier at night, a pilot faces an ultra-short runway at speeds of 180 mph with extremely limited visibility. How does he master his fear?

With traffic zooming all around her, an emergency services doctor has to quickly choose which emergency and trauma cases to treat first. How does she avoid making mistakes?

And what about musicians who improvise in front of large crowds? Tennis players who keep their nerve during match point? Students who are at their best on exam day? All these men and women who have the courage to listen to their inner voices and put their lives on the line, where do they get their self-confidence? What is it that they all have in common?

———

The little girl on her bike can point us in the right direction. There are three places from which she gets her confidence.

First, from her father. She doesn't take off alone, she does it with her father, and thanks to her father. Self-confidence is confidence in someone else.

Then there is her own capability. She has absorbed her father's advice about how to pedal, how to hold the handlebars. She has acquired a skill, without which nothing would be possible. Self-confidence is confidence in one's own abilities.

But there's more. Her bubbling joy as she gathers speed is more than just the satisfaction of knowing how to bicycle. It is a deeper, more encompassing joy, which resonates with gratitude toward life. Self-confidence is confidence in life.

These three drivers of self-confidence will recur—in various forms and to varying degrees—again and again: confidence in others, confidence in one's own capabilities, and confidence in life. That's how it all starts, maybe—when you go at it with the freshness of a child, confident without even knowing what you have confidence in.

"*Confidence is the childish ability* to walk toward something unfamiliar as though recognizing it," Christian Bobin has written. We know more about risks and dangers than when we first hopped on our bikes as children. Our greater understanding makes us more anxious. But it shouldn't blunt our boldness, our ability to go for it. Having confidence in ourselves requires us to keep a child's soul and the mind of an adult.

All of this is forced on us by the times we live in. In traditional societies, every person had his place. You didn't need self-confidence when everything was settled for you at birth, when there was nothing to be conquered. Modern life, on the other hand, makes us free agents, responsible for our own fate. It's our job to get our projects going, to prove our worth, and to build our happiness— our job to invent our own lives. This requires self-confidence.

Yet things are also more complicated than they once were. Self-confidence has never been more important, and it's never been so hard to acquire. Fixing a car engine or building a ladder might once have been a balm to a man's wounds. Feeding one's family entirely with the produce from one's own vegetable garden might once have filled a person's heart with pride. But spending all day in meetings or responding to emails doesn't do the trick. We've lost direct contact with things. Our systems of production are so complicated that we no longer know what it is we do. We follow protocols and processes, but we have a hard time pinpointing our profession. Being as super-connected as we are puts us all at a remove from basic doing and leaves us few concrete opportunities for developing confidence. We need to find a base on which to build our confidence, both personally and collectively.

The journeys taken by Madonna, Patrick Edlinger, George Sand, John Lennon, Serena Williams, and others will give us insight.

We aren't born confident, we become confident. Self-confidence is always something that has to be worked at patiently. It is also something that, once we gain a certain level of effortless command, can give us profound joy.

To probe the mystery of self-confidence, we will look to ancient wisdom and modern philosophers, among them Ralph Waldo Emerson, Friedrich Nietzsche, and Henri Bergson. These thinkers often approach the subject indirectly—it's when they are thinking about freedom, audacity, or individuality that they talk about confidence. We'll also look farther afield, to psychologists like Boris Cyrulnik and psychoanalysts like Jacques Lacan, and to the writings of researchers and teachers. And we'll examine the experiences of athletes, fighter pilots, and emergency room doctors, the words of poets, and the visions of great mystics.

Self-confidence is so central to our existence that it can't be encompassed by a single discipline. We won't learn to understand how it works by studying it in a laboratory. Instead, we'll have to observe self-confidence in real life, watch its birth and development, adopt its rhythm and follow its movement as it hesitates and swerves. We'll have to run alongside it just as you run alongside a child—a child who almost falls, catches herself, and then takes off.

ONE

Cultivate Strong Ties

Confidence through relationships

Gentleness is invincible.
—Marcus Aurelius

Self-confidence first comes from others. This statement might seem paradoxical. It is not. Human infants are extraordinarily fragile and dependent. In their first months of life, they are unable to live on their own. The fact of their survival is proof that they have been cared for by others. Their confidence, first and foremost, is a confidence in their caregivers: self-confidence begins as confidence in others.

It is because we are born at a relatively early stage of fetal development that we need others so much. Embryologists tell us that embryonic cells would require about twenty months to reach maturity. Long ago, Aristotle made the observation that we are born incomplete. It's as though nature had failed to finish its task, propelling us into existence weaker and more unready than any other mammal. We are born not knowing how to walk, a skill that takes a year on average for us to learn. A colt, on the other hand, needs only a few hours, and sometimes only a few minutes, before it starts to gambol. And we should have self-confidence?

We compensate for this natural deficiency through culture—family, mutual assistance, and education. Thanks to our art of human relations, we eventually finish the work that nature left in draft form, and we acquire the confidence that nature withheld from us.

Little by little, children gain confidence, thanks to the ties they develop with others, the care and attention lavished on them, the unconditional love they receive. Small children don't feel that this love is given to them because they try to learn new things or succeed at doing them. They are loved for what they are. This is the most solid base for the self-confidence they will later acquire. Being loved and looked at in this way gives us strength throughout life.

Our struggle to achieve self-confidence starts by overcoming what Freud called infantile anxiety. When adolescents are eager to discover the big wide world or adults have the confidence to manage and launch their projects, it's primarily because they were lucky enough to develop early on, in the course of what Boris Cyrulnik calls their "precocious interactions," the inner security that psychologists have determined is so important.

While self-esteem is based on our assessment of our own value, self-confidence is tied to our capacity for action—our ability to venture forth despite our doubts and take risks in a complex world. To find the courage to venture into the outside world, you have to have inner assurance.

In his masterly essay on the "mirror stage," Jacques Lacan describes the moment at which a child first becomes conscious of himself. When children are still at the toddler stage—the average age is between six and eighteen months—they recognize themselves in the mirror. But what exactly happens that first time? The child is in the arms of an adult, who holds him up to the mirror. No sooner has the child recognized himself than he turns toward the adult and asks him with searching eyes, Is this me? Is it really me? The adult answers with a smile, a look, or a few soothing words. The adult reassures the child: Yes, that's really you. The philosophical implications of this first encounter are enormous— the "other" is there from the outset between me and myself. I am conscious of myself only through that other person. The child has confidence in what he sees in the mirror only because he has confidence in the other. It's in the eyes of others that he seeks this inner reassurance; it's in the eyes of others that he seeks himself.

The same experiment has been tried with rhesus monkeys, which are closely related to us genetically. Their intelligence is apparent in that they quickly start using the mirror to inspect the body parts they can't normally see, such as their backs and buttocks. But on first encountering a mirror, they don't turn toward other rhesus monkeys in the room; they don't look questioningly at their conspecifics. Rhesus monkeys are undoubtedly social animals and learn much from each other, but when it comes to their development they are not as dependent as we on the bonds formed with others; they are not relationship-based creatures to the same extent that humans are. Without others, we humans could not develop our humanity; without others, we could not become what we are.

Look at wild children—those children who have been aban-
doned at birth and raised by animals (bears, wolves, pigs) only
to be found and reintroduced into human society at a later stage.
As François Truffaut's 1970 film *The Wild Child* shows, their
lack of attachment to other humans obstructs their development. They are as frightened as hunted animals, unable to learn
human speech, seemingly irrecoverable to humanity. In the very
best cases, using great patience and gentleness, the professionals
who look after these children have managed to nurture fragile
bonds with them and guide them toward limited progress. But
their self-confidence always remains precarious, vanishing at the
slightest obstacle. In the language of modern psychology, these
wild children suffer from a lack of attachment to other humans.
They never bonded with others during their early childhoods.
They had no one to protect them, reassure them, speak to them,
look at them. Deprived of the inner sense of security that comes
from these attachments, they are unable to muster the minimal
confidence they would need in order to see the world and other
people as anything but hostile.

According to such psychiatrists as John Bowlby and Boris
Cyrulnik, if a little boy of two is able to say hello to a stranger
who comes into his house, smile at him, approach him, and
address or touch him, it's because his sense of inner security
is strong enough to deal with this unfamiliar situation. The
people he has attached to have given him enough confidence
that he can, in fact, move away from them and approach a
stranger.

The education process has been successful when the "student" no longer needs his teachers, when he has enough

self-assurance to leave his teachers behind. By taking a few steps toward the stranger who enters his house, the little boy is already learning to be on his own. Others have shown him confidence, and it's now his turn to act and show he merits it. In order to set off on his own, he draws on the love and attention given to him by his family and those around him.

The first years are decisive, but luckily we can build relationships that give us confidence at any age. If we did not have the good fortune to grow up in a nurturing emotional environment, it's never too late to form the bonds that we lacked early on. But it does require knowing oneself well enough to realize that these bonds are missing and need to be compensated for.

Madonna Louise Ciccone was a shy child who lacked self-confidence. At the age of five, she lost her mother to breast cancer and resented her father's almost immediate remarriage and new set of children. Madonna had trouble finding her place in the family circle. She studied piano and ballet from a young age but felt she wasn't much good at either, that she had to work hard for modest results. But in adolescence, after her stepmother enrolled her in a Catholic school in Detroit, she met Christopher Flynn, a dance teacher who changed her life. While she was rehearsing for the end-of-year show, he said something to her that no one had ever said before, or at least not in so many words: that she was beautiful and talented, and that she had enormous charisma. Years later, Madonna explained that these words changed her life. Before, she hadn't believed in herself. Now, she could see herself as a dancer in

New York; she felt herself being born as an individual. At the end-of-year production, she surprised everyone—her teacher most of all—by dancing with extraordinary energy, and half naked! Madonna was born. Before Christopher Flynn, she'd had dance and piano teachers who had taught her many things, given her insight into movement and technique. But none had ever given her the gift of confidence.

I remember a concert that Madonna gave in Nice, France, when I was not yet eighteen. I was fascinated by her stage presence, her way of singing and dancing, her freedom. I remember the giant screen and her face in close-up when she sang "Like a Prayer." Drops of sweat dripped into her eyes. In the look she gave the audience, in her smile, there seemed to be enormous gratitude. Naturally, Madonna was a highly skilled and experienced performer. The woman striding across the stage in every direction already had years of concerts behind her. But charisma can't be attributed entirely to skill. There's something more, an element of grace that the charismatic person must have. It's in the eyes of others that the charismatic person seeks her own truth; she relates to others through constant reinvention. At the time, I didn't understand very well what I was seeing on that giant screen. Today, when I think back to Madonna's vibrant smile, I believe she was finding in the audience's response, in their energy, even in their love, that same confidence she had seen long before in the eyes of her dance teacher.

Madonna didn't grow up in an environment that gave her security, but she found a way to compensate for it later.

———

If we have had the good fortune in our early years to experience warm and nurturing personal ties, later encounters that reinforce our confidence will still be important. But they will be experienced in a different way: Through them, we will relive, at decisive moments, the grace of someone's early confidence in us.

Yannick Noah, the talented French tennis star, was greatly loved by his parents, Zacharie and Marie-Claire. Deeply in love with each other, they lavished affection on their son. When Yannick was eleven, he met African-American tennis champion Arthur Ashe, who was then ranked fourth in the world. During a tour of Africa, Ashe had stopped for a layover in Yaoundé, Cameroon, where the Noahs were living. Yannick was lucky enough to hit a few balls with Ashe, who was so struck by the youngster's level of play that at the end of the session he gave him his racket. The next day, as Ashe was waiting in the airport to board his plane, the young tennis player ran up to him breathlessly holding out an Arthur Ashe poster for the champion to sign. Ashe did more than give the boy an autograph. He wrote, "See you at Wimbledon!" As Yannick Noah would tell the world a few years later, after having won the men's singles title at the French Open, those four words were an invaluable gift. They galvanized him and stayed with him. They allowed him to believe in his own star; they helped him become a tennis player on a level with Arthur Ashe.

With Madonna and Yannick Noah, we see that sometimes it takes only a few heartfelt words from a teacher or a friend to instill self-confidence, and that those words from the heart can give a person confidence for a lifetime.

———

People can also give us confidence without making lengthy speeches or offering words of encouragement, but by trusting us with a mission.

Once I was visiting a corporation to give a talk on "The Mystery of Confidence." A woman came up to me afterward to say that, upon returning to work after her maternity leave, she lost all her self-confidence, but that she had eventually regained it. The loss had started with her being miserable at having to leave her toddler behind. She felt brittle and on edge and thought she wasn't up to performing her job and assuming its many responsibilities. A few days after her return, her boss called her into his office. She expected the worst. To her surprise, he appointed her to take on a project of crucial importance. No one had ever given her so much responsibility. She immediately regained her self-confidence.

Aristotle provides a very unusual and accurate definition of friendship. A friend, says the author of *The Nicomachean Ethics*, is someone who makes you better. When he or she is around, you feel good, you make progress, you become more intelligent or more sensitive, you open yourself up to new aspects of the world and of yourself—aspects you had not previously known. Friends, says Aristotle, are people who help us "actualize our own power." Thanks to our friends, or more accurately, thanks to the relation that we have with our friends, we develop "in action" talents that had only been latent or "in potential" before. The friendship relation is therefore the occasion for our growth and development. A friend need not be motivated by pure generosity or engaged in listening endlessly to our complaints. If your relation to that person is good for you, for your talent, if it allows you to make progress, then that person is your friend: a friend to the life inside you. From this perspective, the piano or dance or drawing teacher, or the sports champion you happen to meet, or your boss at work can be a friend, on the condition that he or she gives you the opportunity to develop, to make progress.

When we spend time with a martial arts teacher, a sports coach, a yoga instructor—all possible friends in Aristotle's sense—we gain confidence in ourselves, and not just because we are acquiring skills. Sensitive to the positive attention of another, in the company of someone who wants good for us, we rediscover our truth as relational beings. It isn't our piano teacher or our martial arts instructor as such who gives us confidence but the relationship that we have with that person. The relationship is experienced as a series of regular meetings that punctuate the progress we are making. Each time, we feel the other's satisfaction at seeing us improve; we feel the ability that person has to motivate us, to support us when we run into difficulties. Little by little, our mentor's confidence in us becomes our own. That is how confidence works, and it's the human way, properly speaking, to learn.

Good teachers instill confidence in us by making us repeat correct actions, like making us practice our scales. Then they invite us to act on what we have learned: They show confidence in us. When someone makes us feel confident, these two facets are always intertwined.

————

While working on this book, I met a quite unusual mountain climber, Érik Decamp. A graduate of the prestigious École Polytechnique, he had climbed some of the highest peaks in the world, including Ganesh IV in the Himalayas and Shishapangma in Tibet, with his wife, the well-known climber Catherine Destivelle. But he was also an alpine guide, that is, a professional in the field of self-confidence. To practice this profession, you need to have confidence in yourself and you need to be able to impart it to others, to the clients you are guiding. To help a person overcome his fear, Decamp uses a strategy that might seem risky but that often proves very effective. When clients seem particularly nervous during the preparation and training before departure, Decamp will sometimes pick one of them to lead the climb. Often that is enough to free the person of anxiety. Because the guide shows trust in the nervous climber, he or she suddenly feels stronger. Decamp begins instilling confidence by offering advice and explanations and by rehearsing various moves and protocols until they became second nature to his client. Then Decamp proves his trust by asking the chosen climber to lead off. With the others roped in behind him (or her), the designated leader has to show that he is worthy of the confidence that has been placed in him.

Decamp's process is similar to the central precept of Maria Montessori's pedagogical program, which is based on kindliness and trust—and is still being successfully practiced today. "Never help a child with a task at which he feels he can succeed," is a mantra attributed to the great Italian physician and teacher. In other words, trust the student as soon as possible. And placing your trust in a student means not doing the task for her, it means letting her do it herself. We can now understand better why our children are annoyed when, on the pretext of showing them, but often just to make things go faster, we help them do something they can perfectly well do on their own. They are right to be unhappy about it: We have shown that we don't fully trust them.

Every parent, every instructor, every teacher, every friend in Aristotle's sense, should keep in mind this two-pronged method of making someone confident: First instill confidence, then show confidence. First, give them a sense of security, then make them a little insecure. We need both sides to be able to go out into the world. And often, these two dimensions are mingled in the gaze that others train on us: seeing the confidence in their eyes, we feel stronger.

I often experience this in my role as a philosophy teacher and lecturer. Carried away on a flood of words, or deep into a chain of digressions, I can sometimes lose the thread of my argument and come perilously close to having my confidence desert me. But the fact of seeing interest or curiosity in the eyes of my audience is usually enough to get me back on track. Or else I might look at a philosophical text that I have just handed out to my students and find its meaning hopelessly obscure. But as soon as I feel how much confidence they place in me, through the questions they ask, the text becomes much clearer. Érik Decamp told me he has the same experience—as an expedition sets off, the confidence that others have in him reinforces his own. Given that we are animals who depend very much on our relationships, there is nothing surprising here. The two of us, Decamp and I, are like the beginning mountain climbers that he steadies by giving them responsibility: when we feel the confidence that someone else places in us, we rediscover "our own" confidence. Confidence is a gift that others give us, and one that we willingly accept. When my students ask me a difficult question, I offer them a similar gift in return: I tell them that they know the answer. I show that I have confidence in them, and that is usually enough to make them come back quickly with an interesting response.

We sometimes hear that a co-worker, a family member, or someone in the neighborhood lacks self-confidence, as though this confidence were purely an internal matter, something that the person had failed to generate on his or her own. But if no one has ever taken the trouble to give them confidence or placed trust in them, it's not surprising that they suffer from anxiety. People are puzzled that these acquaintances of theirs lack self-assurance, given their abilities. But this is to forget that we are creatures who exist within relationships, not isolated skill-accumulating monads, and that our confidence grows out of the kinds of bonds we have developed with others.

This truth about relational confidence helps us to better understand the suffering of certain oppressed minorities. Often, the most effective method of oppression has been to destroy every kind of bond between individuals and to remove even the possibility of forming interpersonal solidarity. The accounts of enslaved black people and survivors of the Nazi camps illustrate this unequivocally: nothing succeeds in breaking humans better than disrupting the bonds between them, separating families, pitting one against another, and creating a climate of pervasive distrust and denunciation.

In his powerful book *The Fire Next Time*, published in 1963, African-American writer James Baldwin exposes this implacable mechanism of oppression and at the same time confirms that the only way to resist it and maintain one's confidence is to know the value of one's ties to others, to find in them the strength to fight: "Yes, it does indeed mean something—something unspeakable— to be born, in a white country, [...] black. You very soon, without knowing it, give up all hope of communion. Black people, mainly, look down or look up but do not look at each other, not at you, and white people, mainly, look away. And the universe is simply a sounding drum; there is no way, no way whatever, so it seemed then and has sometimes seemed since, to get through a life, to love your wife and children, or your friends, or your mother and father, or to be loved. The universe, which is not merely the stars and the moon and the planets, flowers, grass, and trees, but *other people*, has [...] made no room for you, and if love will not swing wide the gates, no other power will or can."

The psychoanalyst and writer Anne Dufourmantelle, author of *Power of Gentleness* and *L'Éloge du risque* (In praise of risk), who died tragically in 2017 while rescuing two children from drowning, made the radical statement that "there's no such thing as a lack of self-confidence." Listening to the patients on her couch as they tried to find words for their pain, she understood that their anxiety was primarily a lack of confidence in others, the disastrous consequence of a childhood cut off from the precious sense of inner security. The survivors of these unhappy childhoods were so deprived of security and of people who placed trust in them that they were unable to have confidence in themselves. In saying that "there's no such thing as a lack of self-confidence," Dufourmantelle meant that her patients' anxiety derives from a lack of confidence in others. Self-confidence and a confidence in your relationships therefore refer to one and the same thing.

This is similarly illustrated by paranoiacs, who have no confidence in themselves and no confidence in others. Being suspicious of everything that comes from the people around them, from the media, from the world in general, they suffer from "inner insecurity." Consumed by their general mistrust, they can find no basis for having confidence in themselves.

Consequently, to help us develop confidence in ourselves and at the same time have confidence in others, let us venture out, let us establish relations with different and inspiring people, and let us choose teachers and friends who help us grow and who awaken us and reveal us to ourselves. Let us look for relationships that are good for us, that increase our sense of security and thereby free us. And let's remember the little two-year-old: He walks up to the guest who has just entered his house. He advances toward the unknown. He is afraid, obviously. A stranger has just appeared in his house. But he approaches him anyway. He walks forward with his fear. He has confidence in himself, just as he has confidence in the stranger and in the familiar faces around him. This confidence is not genetically or biologically determined. It is developed, little by little, in the intertwining bonds that have enveloped him since birth and reassured him, just like the towels we wrap around infants when they come out of the bath. We sometimes give their little bodies an energetic rub, as if to remind them that we are there, that we are taking care of them, that they are not alone. These attentions give them confidence. This, more than anything, is what they need. Later, when we encourage them to eat by themselves or take their first steps, we will show that we trust them. No one can develop self-confidence all on his or her own. Self-confidence is first and foremost about love and friendship.

TWO

Go into Training

Confidence through practice

Give me a fulcrum, and with my lever I will move the earth.
—Archimedes

As an adolescent, Madonna shook off her inhibitions thanks to the words of her dance teacher. But she already danced well, having studied the art for years. And it was because he had noticed her talent for dance that the teacher singled her out for particular praise. We have stressed the relational component of self-confidence, but we mustn't forget that it also has a great deal to do with skill.

Richard Williams, the father of Venus and Serena Williams, set his daughters on the path to success. He gave them confidence in the best way: he told them he believed in them. He said that thanks to tennis they would rise above their social circumstances, emerge from poverty, and become the best tennis players in the world. But he didn't just voice confidence in them.

He trained them long and hard from the moment they were old enough to hold a racket. The residents of Compton, California, found it fascinating to watch the Williams sisters training: the girls spent their lives on the tennis court, with their father and a basket of balls. Even the gang members in Compton respected the Williams sisters and made sure that no one disrupted their practices. Their father taught them an aggressive style of tennis, starting with a powerful serve and heavy strokes from deep in the backcourt. He coached them to use an attacking strategy, where the point is decided in two or three volleys, a kind of tennis that hadn't existed in the women's game before. He made them hit the same stroke again and again, made them train and train some more, and placed a particular focus on serving—Serena was the first woman to hit a serve clocked at over 124 mph. The sisters did in fact become the best tennis players in the world, one after the other claiming the number one spot in the World Tennis Association rankings. Serena Williams became the best women's tennis player of all time, racking up 39 Grand Slam titles, 23 of them in women's singles events (beating Steffi Graf's record), and 12 in doubles with her older sister, including one when she was two months pregnant! In the history of tennis, she is the only player to have won a Grand Slam title after saving match point in the finals. And she has done it three times! It takes astonishing confidence not to falter in the finals of a major tournament when you are facing match point.

This confidence came from her tennis skills, a product of her intense training. But it doesn't just come down to skill. Thanks to repeating the same gestures over and over, they had become second nature to her. Her extreme skill in the end became part of her personality: in Serena Williams's case, expertise seems to have transformed into confidence. Does this always happen?

In a book that has become a worldwide success, *Outliers*, Malcolm Gladwell attacks the idea of innate talent and argues for the seductive "10,000-hour rule," generalizing an idea originally developed by the psychologist Anders Ericsson. Examining the careers of a group of violinists who trained together at the Berlin Academy of Music, Ericsson wondered what accounted for the stratification of the students, who were all excellent musicians. The very best became first violinists in prestigious orchestras or soloists with international careers; the very good ones became professional musicians; and the rest became "only" music teachers. He asked them all the same question: "Since the time when you first took up the violin, how many hours have you played?" The results surprised him. By the age of twenty, none of those who would go on to become "just" music teachers had played his or her instrument for more than 4,000 hours. All those who would become highly qualified professional musicians had played and practiced on their instrument for about 8,000 hours. And the highest achievers, those who would become stars in the violin world, had all played for more than 10,000 hours. There wasn't a single exception. Anders Ericsson then repeated his research with pianists and came up with similar results: professional pianists had about 8,000 hours of playing under their belts, while virtuosos had at least 10,000 hours. He didn't find a single case of a musician who became a virtuoso without passing the 10,000-hour mark (which works out to roughly three hours a day for ten years).

I am a great fan of the saxophone improvisations of Sonny Rollins: they strike me as a symbol of pure confidence. Rollins ventures down paths that no one else has explored and creates heavenly, dream-like ballads of astonishing freedom. Recently, I came across an interview with Rollins where he described playing the saxophone at some points in his life for up to seventeen hours a day. His confidence was achieved with a huge amount of work. He had to practice scales on his instrument and master its techniques before he could improvise with such freedom. Among great artists, confidence comes above all from constant, devoted, almost obsessional practice.

But the results of Anders Ericsson's study should not be interpreted in a simplistic way. Not everyone is going to become a virtuoso just by sticking to an instrument for 10,000 hours. You need to take pleasure in the activity, which has to align with your aspirations, and have a basic predisposition for music. And you need to be attentive during those 10,000 hours— truly present to your art. Other factors probably enter into it as well. The study is interesting all the same because, through its different gradations, it shows how a skill can gradually be incorporated to become genuine confidence. After 8,000 hours, my capabilities are at the point where I can become a professional. Once I have passed the 10,000-hour mark, I can entertain the ambition of becoming one of the best in the world in my field. When Serena Williams became the number one female player in the under-ten age group, she in fact had 10,000 hours of playing behind her.

Malcolm Gladwell took Anders Ericsson's study and made it into a general law, as well as a bestseller with a whiff of demagoguery about it. Gladwell suggests that in any given field, you need only practice for 10,000 hours in order to acquire mastery of your art and full confidence in yourself. He analyzed the accomplishments of many people in great detail, including those of Mozart and the Beatles, showing that in every case, true excellence was achieved only after crossing the 10,000-hour threshold. It's true, of course, that Mozart could follow a score and play to tempo even before he knew how to read or write. And it's true that he started composing at the age of six. But his first masterpiece, according to Gladwell—his *Piano Concerto No. 9 in E-flat Major*, K.271—was written in Salzburg in 1777. Mozart was twenty-one at the time and already had 10,000 hours of composing to his credit.

Reexamining the history of the Beatles before their wildly successful tour of the United States in 1964, Gladwell counts how many hours John Lennon and Paul McCartney spent playing music onstage. He tells how, in 1960, when they were a schoolboys' rock and roll band, they were lucky enough to be asked to play at a club in Hamburg. The sets at the Hamburg club lasted eight hours at a stretch, and sometimes all night. This was playing on a different scale from the band's practices in Liverpool, which had lasted an hour at most and often involved repeating the same few songs over and over. In Gladwell's telling, the Hamburg club gave the Beatles a chance to really train, and it was there that they gained confidence in themselves, especially in their ability to perform together onstage. The many hours of playing allowed them to learn their instruments thoroughly, to expand their repertoire, and to explore their vocal range. It was also there that they learned to read their public and bring it to a pitch of excitement. The Hamburg experience made them a great band. When they landed in the United States in 1964, they had already spent—according to Gladwell's detailed calculations—some 12,000 hours onstage. That's what allowed them to win the hearts of Americans.

Clearly, Anders Ericsson's findings are not, strictly speaking, scientific: his theory that excellence can be achieved in any field with 10,000 hours of practice is neither verifiable nor refutable. And when Gladwell uses the work of neuroscientist Daniel Levitin to support the thesis that 10,000 hours is the time it takes the brain to master any discipline, he seems to be reaching for scientific validation. There are many reasons to be wary of this thesis. But I have to admit I find it quite seductive. It makes us realize that even among geniuses, confidence takes time to achieve. Confidence develops in tandem with a growing competence that, as it becomes integrated in stages and incorporated, has a liberating effect. Confidence is not innate but something that is largely acquired.

"Genius," as Thomas Edison put it, "is 1 percent inspiration and 99 percent perspiration." We shouldn't forget this when we start to have doubts about ourselves. Often, when our confidence is at a low ebb, we start to think that we lack talent or aren't good at what we do, when in fact it's just a matter of not having trained enough. Whenever doubt starts to gain the upper hand, whenever we're afraid that we won't measure up, the best thing to do is to bolster our confidence by actively developing our skills, rather than invoking some hypothetical lack of talent. Gladwell's unusual book reminds us of this: Mozart was perhaps an inspired genius, but he also perspired a great deal. He even perspired considerably more than many musicians less inspired than he. Keeping this in mind can help us draw strength from his example.

But Gladwell is only interested in a very localized confidence, focused on the skill to which 10,000 hours of practice have been devoted. True self-confidence, on the other hand, is much broader in its extent. It goes beyond the mastery of a single discipline, even if that mastery contributes to it.

Through her skill at tennis and the great success it has brought her, Serena Williams has acquired a sense of confidence that is not limited to the tennis court. When she makes her voice heard nowadays, it is no longer just as a high-ranking sports figure but as a woman, a mother, a citizen, and a feminist. And her voice finds a wide audience.

In 2016, Williams published an open letter denouncing sexism in sports and the persistent inequality between the sexes. Here is an excerpt:

> *What others marked as flaws or disadvantages about myself—my race, my gender—I embraced as fuel for my success. I never let anything or anyone define me or my*

potential.... Women have to break down many barriers on the road to success. One of those barriers is the way we are constantly reminded we are not men, as if it is a flaw. People call me one of the "world's greatest female athletes." Do they say LeBron is one of the world's best male athletes? Is Tiger? Federer? Why not? ... We should never let this go unchallenged. We should always be judged by our achievements, not by our gender.

Serena's confidence is also a transformation of her prowess. By training for all those years, day after day, by hitting balls for hours, she didn't just train at tennis. On a daily basis, she showed her strength of will, her hunger for achievement, her ability to overcome obstacles. The confidence that now allows her to take courageous positions is the fruit of that experience. As she developed her skill at hitting serves, as she worked on her forehand and her backhand, she became aware of her own power and her drive for life—on the tennis court and everywhere else. By playing tennis, she discovered her own truth; she reached deep within herself and found remarkable resources.

By developing our range within a discipline, we are fortunately able to gain a broader self-confidence. Our experience in that discipline, whatever it may be, can then serve as a fulcrum. "Give me a fulcrum, and with my lever I can move the earth," said Archimedes. Because our self-confidence plays an important role in how we act, how we engage with the world, everything that anchors us to reality can serve as a base and a springboard.

———

"All consciousness is consciousness of something," said the German philosopher Edmund Husserl. He meant that we become conscious of ourselves by being conscious of something other than ourselves. For example, because I am conscious of the taste of coffee in my mouth and of the cup I'm holding in my hand, I am conscious of myself. But I am not conscious of myself in a pure, abstract, or disembodied way.

The same goes for self-confidence. In order to feel confidence in ourselves, we must first feel confidence based on specific actions. To paraphrase Husserl, we could say, "all self-confidence is confidence in the accomplishment of something." We need concrete experiences, specific skills, and real successes in order to have confidence in ourselves. So let's not hesitate to celebrate our successes, even the small ones—they are so many stages along the way to full-blown self-confidence. We sense this when we congratulate our children: we are inviting them each time to have a little more confidence in themselves.

During childhood, we developed confidence in our ability to put one foot in front of the other, to write in cursive, to ride a bike. As adults, we might have confidence in our ability to read a score, to find our way around a foreign city, to start a conversation, to express our disagreement, to formulate what it is that we want, to speak in public...

And then one day, we have confidence in ourselves.

That's what I call the leap in self-confidence. All the other actions we take are so many paths leading to this leap and making it possible, so many opportunities for experiencing this metamorphosis. There is no point, as it happens, in wanting to hasten its arrival: we don't gain more confidence in ourselves by seeking it out insistently. You have to practice your scales patiently, with your curiosity aroused. And one day, almost without realizing it, you start to improvise.

By what miracle does a particular capability lead to true confidence? There are in fact skills that exist behind a wall, that never morph into self-confidence. Serena Williams is a model of one kind, but there are many excellent tennis players who aren't able to assert themselves beyond the tennis court. Psychologists are aware of the problem: our confidence is often compartmentalized, limited to a skill set that we have mastered. Or worse, sometimes we do not even have confidence in ourselves in the field where we've gained mastery. We have mastered it, but we are trembling inside. What is the best way to turn competence into confidence?

The first step is to take pleasure in developing that competence. I see this with my students every day: there is nothing like pleasure to help a student develop his or her abilities and acquire confidence. Those who find a kind of enjoyment in staking out the parameters of a problem and constructing their arguments make much better progress than those who think that serious work has to be performed with a serious attitude. Those who relish the process escape the strict logic of competence and are quicker to have confidence in themselves. The reason is simple: taking pleasure in what they are doing lets them step back and be more relaxed. If they make a mistake, at least they will have had fun. And in fact, they make fewer mistakes when they are enjoying the work they do. The pleasure we feel in such circumstances is an indication that the field of study suits us and that we stand to gain by delving deeper into it. It's reassuring to know that we are pursuing a path that is congenial to us.

Competence is therefore more likely to turn into confidence when it helps us to reach a greater knowledge of ourselves, our resources and characteristics, our tastes and distastes, and more. No lasting self-confidence is possible unless we know ourselves, unless we are plowing a furrow that corresponds to our own nature. In learning to play tennis, Serena Williams discovered what she was capable of, what her strengths and her weaknesses were, what kind of woman she was. She understood she was the kind of person who becomes her truest self in moments of adversity.

As soon as our skill or ability tells us something about ourselves, we are no longer locked within the strict logic of competence. When our ability is compartmentalized, it doesn't help us overcome our anxieties. If we develop a skill thinking that it will give us a broad power over the unexpected, we run the risk of having our confidence shaken when something truly unexpected happens. Life is all too good at confounding our forecasts. If we increase our mastery with the illusion that it will give us total control, we are setting ourselves up for disappointments that will undermine our confidence. We have to develop our mastery while recalling that we will not be able to master everything, that things never repeat themselves identically.

"We never step twice into the same river," says a fragment from the teachings of Heraclitus. Even if our skill level is very high, the second time something happens is never an exact repetition of the first. A surgeon may have a thorough knowledge of the actions he needs to perform, the tools, and the timing, but he must deal each time with a new human body, identical overall but individual in its particulars and therefore different. His skill allows him to deal with any novel aspects; it is layered and extensive enough that he can adapt to any unforeseen features of a case. Serena Williams may be extraordinarily skilled, but the first time she saved match point in the finals of a Grand Slam tournament, it was very much her first time doing it. And the two other times were not identical reconstructions of the first. If the surgeon and Serena Williams manage to come up with the right reaction, it's because they can draw on their great skill. They perform actions that they had mastered perfectly. But they do more than that. They perform them without a tremor, although they are not simply repeating a gesture mechanically. They are able to be inventive, to adapt to the situation, even if minimally, and that's what makes all the difference.

In Thus Spake Zarathustra, *Nietzsche imagines* a grotesque character, the Conscientious One, to illustrate the difference between competence that walls a person off and experience that gives freedom. In Nietzsche's view, it all hinges on what we have "in the pit of our stomach" when we set out to develop competence.

If we are driven solely by the "instinct of fear," if we are working toward expertise because we are afraid of the unknown, then we will never draw true confidence from it. We will be skillful but not confident, and we will be like the sinister Conscientious One. An expert of sorts, a pathetic version of the researcher, he knows everything, absolutely everything, about the brain of the leech, but his great competence in his chosen field cuts him off from life, since nothing else interests him. His unusual expertise will eventually kill him, in a surreal scene that displays Nietzsche's comic genius. Falling into a marsh swarming with leeches, the Conscientious One will be sucked dry of his own blood, devoured by the very object of his expertise.

Fortunately, we can take the opposite approach to expertise, using what Nietzsche calls the "instinct of art," a form of creativity that he contrasts with the "instinct of fear." It will allow us to extend and develop the life within us, not run away from it. It will make us more alive, not less so. Our actions will be guided by curiosity, not the instinct to ball up into a cocoon. Naturally, we harbor both these instincts within us, the fear instinct and the art instinct. Each time that the art instinct wins out over the fear instinct, each time that our creativity wins out over our instinct to curl up into a ball, we make it more likely that competence will translate into confidence.

Let us take Zarathustra's advice: let us develop our abilities, but with the soul of an artist, and let us use our abilities as a springboard, not a palisade. Our skills and our areas of strength, reassure us, certainly, but let's not forget the goal of this reassurance, which is to come out of our comfort zone and have confidence in ourselves. If we work on our abilities with the aim of finding complete reassurance, we will not be able to have true confidence in ourselves, for a reason that Nietzsche diagnosed with pitiless accuracy. Life is unpredictable, at times unfair, and, when you come right down to it, anxiety-producing. As long as we remain lucid, we will never live with complete reassurance.

Our competence, then, must be more than the ability to repeat what we already know how to do. It must become the field in which our creativity develops, the occasion for us to be present to our true selves. This change is possible only as the upshot of a long and slow process: mastery leads us gradually to the acceptance of a kind of "nonmastery," of letting go. Thanks to everything we have learned, experienced, and integrated, we give ourselves the permission to have confidence in ourselves.

Serena Williams started playing tennis at the age of three. Her feet, as she sat on the courtside bench, didn't reach the ground. She learned the different tennis strokes, gradually hitting them better and better until her competence rose to a very high level. But when, in three separate finals, she had to save match point and did so without a tremor, she didn't just have confidence in her strokes, she had confidence in herself. From repetition, her competence was incorporated into her and became second nature. The leap that I spoke of had occurred, and her competence had become confidence.

This leap remains somewhat mysterious. But there is one thing we do know: to accomplish such a leap, we need to regularly reimmerse ourselves in our mastery so as to courageously take a step into "nonmastery." We must reassure ourselves in our comfort zone first so we will then be able to leave it.

Think of your comfort zone, or your area of competence, as a circle. You go into it to soak up warmth. Then you leave it to explore the big world beyond. You come back to it to be reassured again. And so on. Compose yourself inside your comfort zone, only to reemerge from it each time. Dancing. Moving forward. Enlarging both the circle of your comfort zone and the boundaries of your exploration. To a rhythm. This dance step, this two-time waltz, gives us a model for the way self-confidence operates. Each person has to know himself well enough to sense how often he will need to reimmerse himself in his comfort zone. The less security we received in childhood, the more often we will need to reassure ourselves. You have to know yourself well to find the rhythm that works for you, to find your dance.

My students acquire various abilities and master certain concepts that are part of the curriculum. As the time approaches for them to take the baccalaureate exam, they sometimes get nervous at the thought of all the topics we haven't covered. They ask me to give lectures or distribute handouts on the skipped concepts. I urge them instead to review the ones they have already mastered; to reread the lectures they liked; to reexperience pleasure, which is the best ally of confidence. In a word, I tell them to reimmerse themselves in their comfort zone. And afterward, but only afterward, to go out and discover new concepts. I invite them to dance this two-time waltz.

I also advise them to get in training by writing short introductions or essays. "It's by blacksmithing that you become a blacksmith," says a medieval proverb. Even Hephaestus, the god of blacksmiths, didn't become a blacksmith overnight. Because of his ugliness, his parents threw him into the sea when he was born. He was rescued by nymphs, who raised him and, over the years, taught him the art of blacksmithing. Hephaestus, the god of the forge, had to put in at least 10,000 hours of practice! I ask my students to train, but I also warn them against the idea that by increasing their skills they will automatically get a better result—the topic they are given on the baccalaureate exam is not likely to resemble any topic that has come up before. This is one of the chief difficulties of being a teacher: you must instill competence in your students, while paradoxically teaching them to mistrust competence in and of itself.

The students who train with fear in their bellies, anxious to be prepared for any topic, will never achieve true self-confidence. They acquire abilities that will win them some success as scholars, but they will continue to lack self-confidence and trip up at some point or other. They will be more prone to panic on the day of the big exam when faced with an unexpected question. They put too much faith in their abilities and not enough in themselves.

On the other hand, there are students who train in the spirit of discovery and are less intent on scholarship per se. They are not as obsessed with being perfectly prepared and are more likely to try things and respond to challenges. They aren't looking to reassure themselves at all costs. They turn to their studies with a sense of pleasure, being creative about it. They don't talk about topics in quite the same way as the others—there is excitement in their voices, and an active curiosity crowds out their anxiety. The results are striking. While the first group of students is terrified by the uncertainty that is part of any exam, the second thinks of it as fun. They are ready to deal with what's served up to them. They understand that this is integral to human life.

Confidence is not the same thing as reassurance. To have confidence in yourself is to know that you can handle the unexpected, not to mistakenly believe that life is foreseeable. It's true that there are situations where a high degree of competence reduces the risk of the unexpected almost to nothing, but in those cases you don't really need confidence in yourself—competence is enough.

In his essay Oser faire confiance (*Daring to trust*), the philosopher Emmanuel Delessert explains the difference between confidence and competence: "Having confidence in oneself does not mean being certain one can do something because one has already done it a thousand times—how sad! How limited! On the contrary, it means turning to that uncertain part of oneself—which has never yet been activated—and electing to call on it, to wake it up." To trust ourselves is to undertake something we haven't "already done a thousand times," something that we may never have tried before. When we succeed, it isn't just our competence that gives us confidence; it's ourselves.

———

"*The experience of others* is a comb for a bald man," says a witty Chinese proverb. What does it mean? That only our own experiences count, not other people's, because only our own experiences can give us confidence. Like "a comb for a bald man," someone else's experience isn't of much use to us. At most, it adds a little to our competence. But what's more important than our competence is the path we have traveled and how we've negotiated it, which together make up our true experience and our treasure. Along the way, we have learned about how we react to adversity, failure, or success; we've taken the measure of our talent, our desire, our ambition. We've gained in self-knowledge. No one can walk this road for us.

A striking illustration of how an ability acquired from long effort can give rise to true confidence can be found in Frederick Douglass's memoir, *Narrative of the Life of Frederick Douglass, an American Slave, Written by Himself.* "You have seen how a man was made a slave; you shall see how a slave was made a man," Douglass wrote, in a text that is both a gripping account of slavery and a powerful work of literature. A man is made into a slave by cutting him off from his close family while he is still an infant; by reducing him to a commodity that is weighed on a scale, traded, and sold in the marketplace; by exposing him to the arbitrary will of his masters and the casual cruelty of their whips; and finally, by depriving him of the slightest information that would allow him to know who he is: his age, his name, the identity of his parents. "By far the larger part of the slaves know as little of their age as horses know of theirs," wrote Douglass, "and it is the wish of most masters within my knowledge to keep their slaves thus ignorant." But Douglass also shows how, from being a slave, he managed to become a man and have confidence in himself, have confidence in life, despite the vast machinery of dehumanization put in place by the slave system. In these astonishing pages, he talks of all the stratagems he resorted to and the hiding places he used each time he transgressed against the rules of slavery by teaching himself how to read, and then to write. He would decipher letters chalked on pieces of wood in order to learn the alphabet, and he exchanged bread stolen from home for "the valuable bread of knowledge" from the poor but literate white boys he met in the street. He would steal newspapers at the risk of being brutally whipped or sold to a master even more savage than his own. His progress was slow but steady. In following it, we see how his mind opened little by little to the world, how this gradual decipherment brought him joy, and how this growing skill gave him confidence. In these extreme conditions, self-confidence is first felt as a confidence that comes from a specific set of actions and from repetition, which allows people to measure their progress and establish a point of anchorage in the world. Obviously, Douglass's apprenticeship to the practice of reading and writing had nothing in common with his apprenticeship to the work on the cotton plantation. The repetitiveness of the work Douglass experienced while enslaved on a plantation was painful, and it alienated him from himself. But when he worked at learning to read and write, the repetition gave him joy and made him more conscious of himself. By training to decipher letters and then words, Frederick Douglass was in fact training himself for freedom. And when we read his book, magnificently written in eleven short but densely packed chapters, we are holding in our hands the work of a man who became confident of his freedom, little by little, step by step, by learning to read and write.

The distinction that Nietzsche proposed is particularly illuminating here: on the one hand, a dully performed repetition, cut off from life, that gradually saps a person's vitality; and on the other, a liberating repetition, filled with life, leading to growth. On one side is a competence that sucks life dry; on the other, a competence that nourishes life and gives confidence.

Develop your competence, skills, and abilities as much as you can, but without tensing up. Always make sure that your growing competence brings you closer in touch with yourself and allows you to find your freedom. Develop your abilities to the greatest extent possible, but without letting them take over. Confidence will come as an added benefit. Like grace, it comes as a reward and a surprise.

THREE

Listen to Yourself

Trusting your intuition

A man should learn to detect and watch that gleam of light
that flashes across his mind from within.
—Ralph Waldo Emerson

Among the medical technicians who provide emergency care, the
on-call physician has to sort out absolute emergencies from relative ones. While sirens wail and the wounded cry out around her,
she has to triage the patients, evaluating at a glance the gravity
of their conditions, from the color of their cheeks, the whites of
their eyes, and the movement of their chests. You have to be confident in your judgment to make decisions in a crisis, to listen to
yourself in the midst of the tumult. The emergency doctor has to
stay calm and immediately make good decisions. How does she do
it? Does she analyze the situation coldly? It wouldn't be enough,
because she doesn't have the time to analyze everything. Does she
act on instinct, trusting her previous experience? That wouldn't

be enough either, because she needs data, clinical information. In fact, she is invested in the decision as a whole person, her emotions, reasoning mind, body, and spirit.

A business executive is in the thick of a heated negotiation. The back and forth has been going on for some time, but suddenly he "feels" it. He changes his tone and proposes a final price. Take it or leave it. After a few seconds, his counterpart accepts. The executive's intuition was right. He knew how to listen to himself. And to listen to his whole self. At the moment when he proposes his final price, he, too, is entirely present to himself and to the situation. It would be wrong to think that he does nothing more than analyze the situation coldly and make rapid calculations. It would be just as wrong to think that he works purely on his emotions, interpreting the other's body language. He does all of that at the same time, and that's why he feels it. In past negotiations, he has known failures as well as successes. He doesn't make an effort to forget his failures and remember his successes. Otherwise, he couldn't be truly present in the situation. He knows how to be the sum of all that he has lived through, to welcome the entirety of his experience in the moment, so that he is able to quote the right price. The ability to listen to yourself is at once simple and complicated. Simple, because it doesn't require any gift. Complicated, because it's hard to achieve this extreme degree of presence in the heat of the moment, during an emergency, or at a time of great pressure.

————

If this capacity to listen to ourselves depended on the extraordinary development of one or another aspect of our make-up, we might worry about never being able to achieve it. But it doesn't require anything of the sort. Rather, it's a question of letting all the parts of ourselves speak in concert: reason and sensibility, the conscious mind and the unconscious. To truly listen to ourselves, the important thing is for none of our faculties to predominate over the others. If our reason dominates, then we'll obey our reason. If our emotions take over, we'll follow them. When none of our faculties overshadows the others, then what we listen to and have confidence in is ourselves. We are all capable of doing this.

All too often when we were in school, we were told to pay attention to the rules, the regulations, the classroom lessons. We were asked to listen to our teachers. We were never told that the whole point was to be able to listen to ourselves.

Studies conducted by the Programme for International Student Assessment, an organization that compares the educational systems of different countries, have shown that French students register a glaring disparity between their level of knowledge and their performance on multiple-choice exams. They know a lot, but when it comes to deciding between several answers, they hesitate and choose the wrong one at a higher-than-average rate. Why do French youths get more rattled than the youths of other European countries when faced with boxes to check? Because they haven't learned to listen to themselves. All too rarely do our school reports include the words "trust yourself." The comment that the student "can do better" or that he "must persevere in his efforts" is common enough, but how often do we see "have more confidence in your own judgment"?

I was lucky enough to have two teachers who changed the course of my life. In my literature class, in tenth grade, I discovered Paul Verlaine, Marcel Proust, Albert Camus, and others. My teacher was very old-school and very demanding, making us learn poems by heart. But she never failed to ask us about our own feelings, to invite us to listen to ourselves: "Yes, you're right, you could certainly say that, but what about you, what do you think about it? Do you think it's well written? How does it affect you?"

My philosophy professor introduced me to Aristotle, Baruch Spinoza, G. W. F. Hegel, and other giants of Western thought. He taught me a great deal, introducing me to new ideas and methods. But more than anything, he taught me to listen to myself. He too would often respond, in biting tones, even after giving a long lecture on René Descartes: "For God's sake, stop with the Descartes! What do *you* think about it?" Twenty-five years later, what I remember about the hours I spent in philosophy class is that they were hours "for me," set aside from the hurly-burly of life, the demands of daily living, and family responsibilities: hours spent learning to listen to myself. In philosophy class, we read Plato, Immanuel Kant, and Jean-Paul Sartre in order to come back to ourselves. We entered Hegel's *Phenomenology of Mind* only to learn how better to listen to our own minds.

Great teachers launch you into the adventure of life. They give you the tools to be yourself. Often, we feel that they have traveled a road analogous to our own—they, too, became themselves by coming into contact with the authors and ideas they are now teaching. They are the opposite of the Conscientious One whom Nietzsche mocked, the kind of person who becomes a teacher because he is afraid of life, because he lacks confidence in himself. This frightened teacher and others like him were once dedicated students and have now gone around to the far side of the desk. But did they listen to themselves? What did they learn about themselves? Do they know what their attitude as obedient students said about their relationship to the world? These are the teachers who humiliate their students at the least infraction of the rules, at the slightest sign of levity, undermining their students' confidence with slashes of their red ballpoints.

When I think back to these two teachers of mine, I also remember that they had the courage to say simple things, which sometimes even struck me as simplistic. I would understand it later: where others camouflaged the little they had to say in pretentious jargon, they knew how to express very complex ideas in a simple way. Having the courage to speak simply requires the courage to listen to yourself. There is no better way to make a student want to listen to himself, whether he is in grade school, high school, or college, than to show him this virtue in action. I can't think of anything better that a person can be taught in school. Listen to your teachers: they will teach you to listen to yourself.

———

But listening to yourself is never that easy. You first need to stop accepting conventional truths. If these truths derive from religion or social tradition, they can be openly debated and questioned. Someone who unquestioningly repeats what his religious education has taught him about God won't be able to listen to himself: he will never know whether he truly believes or not. The person who says, "We've always done things that way here," in order to avoid an open discussion has also given up any chance of listening to himself. He is submitting to the "truth" of tradition just as others submit to the "truth" of religion. He venerates the past too much to really trust himself. He can't conceive that what is unfolding within himself, here and now, has the weight of authority.

If the conventional truths are being propounded by science, we should still want to understand how they were arrived at. Knowing how to listen to yourself is a matter of integrating knowledge and remembering to question it.

Knowing how to listen to yourself also means not giving in to a sense of urgency. We all know how that happens: We're short on time, or afraid of being late, or in a stressful situation, and we act in an abrupt, rushed way. We obey the person who is hurrying us the most, who is shouting the loudest, and we become, as it were, absent to ourselves. We are no longer able to hear our inner voice.

One of the ways to free ourselves from the tyranny of urgency is to make the distinction between urgency and importance. Many things are urgent, but not all are important. Simply remembering this distinction can sometimes be liberating, and it doesn't stop us from continuing to do what we need to do in a limited amount of time. Many executives, who are constantly under time pressure, lose confidence in their own judgment. But we can always counter the incessant flood of demands, each more urgent than the last, by asking this simple question: Granting the urgency, is it important? What is truly important in our professional lives is that we do the things we have to do, as defined by the terms of our job, and that we do them well. With this in mind, we can try to satisfy the urgent request of a colleague or boss, but armed with a new inner freedom. It may be that this colleague or boss is himself overcome by stress, and that he is putting undue pressure on us or asking us for things that are not really in our purview. It then behooves us not to lose sight of what is important: doing what we need to do well. We can also frame this distinction between the urgent and the important in a larger perspective, not limiting it to our professional lives. What is important is that our children should prosper and be in good spirits, that we are spared life's tragedies, and that we know how to make the best of life. Then, even when we are in a rush at the office, we know that the essential lies elsewhere. We are in a hurry, but we are not being *dictated to* by the urgency of the situation. By remembering the difference between urgency and importance, we can maintain the ability to listen to ourselves.

The emergency services doctor also has to act in a hurry. The flood that assails her is not a flood of emails but a flood of trauma cases. She acts with urgency, but has an inner compass. She doesn't let herself be affected by the commotion all around her. She knows that some emergencies are more important than others. She isn't caught up in the high-speed tempo of the environment in which she works. She draws her serenity from a longer time span, the time during which she accumulated the experiences that now allow her to listen to herself in an emergency so that she can perform the most important actions, those that will save the maximum number of lives.

The only philosopher to have seriously addressed the question of self-confidence is Ralph Waldo Emerson, born in Boston, Massachusetts, in the early nineteenth century. In his essay "Self-Reliance," published in 1841, he seems to draw a portrait of our emergency services doctor: "It is easy in the world to live after the world's opinion; it is easy in solitude to live after our own; but the great man is he who in the midst of the crowd keeps with perfect sweetness the independence of solitude." Even when surrounded by a crowd, the person who has self-confidence knows how to listen to himself or herself as though alone in a quiet place. The experienced frontline doctors and emergency medics are proof of the greatness Emerson describes: They make good decisions because they maintain a kind of independence; they have an aptitude for being present to themselves in the midst of chaos. "A man," Emerson continues, "should learn to detect and watch that gleam of light that flashes across his mind from within, more than the lustre of the firmament of bards and sages."

Managing to listen to ourselves doesn't happen on its own. It is something that is learned, often with the help of rituals that are a kind of appointment with oneself. Rituals help us preserve a certain distance from the hysteria of the times and the break-neck pace of our lives. They help us get back in touch with our inner selves. To stretch out twice a week on a psychoanalyst's couch; to go running three times a week; to practice meditation, or yoga, or shintaido regularly; to keep the Sabbath on Friday; to attend Mass on Sunday or mosque on Friday—each of these rituals can provide us with a framework for listening to ourselves. They take us out of the urgent hubbub to re-center ourselves on what is important. We can recover our breath, become mindful of ourselves again, and we may often find, in these moments, that constricting knots are untied. We solve the problem in our professional lives that has long been bedeviling us, we understand what we have been looking for in our love life, and we see ourselves more clearly. The light often comes on during our moments of downtime. We then understand that we can have confidence in ourselves: the answer was inside us all along. We just needed a structure to help us become aware of it.

It has happened to me so many times—I'll be lying on the analyst's couch, talking. Just as the Freudian theory of free association describes, I'll be saying things as they come to me, when suddenly a piece of the puzzle will pop into place. I'll see something that I hadn't noticed before, that I hadn't wanted to see. I'll suddenly understand why I react the way I do, why I get nervous, or why I feel relief. I'm not repressing memories to try to convince myself of something. I'm not ignoring my body in order to listen to my conscience. I am entirely present. I'd forgotten that I even knew how to enter this state. We all have a talent for lying to ourselves, and we're very good at not listening to our inner voice. That is the reason why I suffered a severe depression, years ago, and discovered psychoanalysis. I emerged from my depression fairly quickly, but I continued to visit the analyst's couch. It's a ritual that I need. It gives me a chance to stop, a framework where I don't have to lie, where I finally manage to listen to myself.

In The Little Prince, *the children's book* by Antoine de Saint-Exupéry, the fox reproaches the prince for having returned to visit him at a different time every day, without developing a ritual:

> "It would be better to come back at the same time," said the
> fox. "If, for example, you always came at four o'clock in the
> afternoon, at three o'clock I would begin to be happy. And I
> would feel happier and happier as the hour advanced. At four
> o'clock I would already be restless and worried; I would be
> discovering the cost of happiness! But if you come at any time,
> I will never know when to prepare my heart for you... Rituals
> are necessary."
>
> "What is a ritual?" asked the little prince.
>
> "It is something else that is too often forgotten," said the
> fox. "It's what makes one day different from other days, one
> hour different from other hours."

"Rituals are necessary," says the fox. Without them, we would always have to count on our will to supply us with those moments of letting go, of being present to ourselves. If I have an appointment with the psychoanalyst every Tuesday and Thursday at 7:00 PM, then I don't need to make an effort of will to bring it about. It has become a ritual. If I attend Mass every Sunday at 11:00 AM, it costs me no special effort to get to church. The ritual supports me: it takes the place of an effort of will. If our will always had to win out over practical concerns and our innate resistance, we would end up on the analyst's couch once a month and at Mass once a year.

Thanks to rituals, the fox aptly notes, "one day is different from other days." Because rituals are repeated, they allow us to take account of what is not repeated: they help us understand our progress along the path of life. Without these regular stops, how would we know the pace at which we are moving? Let us be wary of unstructured lives, and let us become reacquainted with the sense of ritual that modern life has eroded.

In the highly structured world of pre-Revolutionary France, the lives of men and women were certainly much more ritualized, but a person's ability to listen to himself or herself wasn't valued. In fact, it posed a threat to societal norms and risked unnecessary disruption in a hierarchically structured society. Why place confidence in individuals when what was needed for society to function was that individuals simply submit to tradition and established norms? Why invite them to listen to themselves when all knowledge was known to derive from the sages of antiquity and all decisions were in the hands of princes? Self-confidence had no real meaning in the pre-Revolutionary world, except as it applied to a few aristocrats with a chivalric turn of mind. Self-confidence is a modern concept, an upshot of democratic ideals and the writings of the Enlightenment philosophers. "Have the courage to rely on your own understanding. That is the Enlightenment motto," wrote Kant. This invitation to make use of one's own mind is nothing other than an invitation to listen to oneself.

Trusting your intuition and learning to listen to yourself are just a part of being free. When we take shelter behind pseudo-truths, when we submit to the ideas of those "in the know," we are failing to assume our freedom. Sartre's name for this renunciation was "bad faith." Good faith, by contrast, is confidence in our freedom. We often think of freedom in the wrong way, equating it with a total lack of external constraints. Since our lives are constrained in one way or another, we deduce that we are not free.

In fact, freedom has nothing to do with lack of constraints. We are free, according to the French philosopher Henri Bergson, when we are fully what we are, when we manage to bring together in the present moment the totality of our past, all our experiences. That is exactly what listening to oneself is. Being mindful of one's past, one's lived experience, is not the same as simplifying it into a unified fiction or a procrustean identity but accepting it as is, in its irreducible complexity. We are free when we manage to listen to ourselves in our entirety. The emergency services doctor in the thick of the action is not free of external constraints, in fact she is caught in a web of overlapping constraints. Yet she is free in Bergson's sense: she is entirely herself at the heart of the action.

And we can't be free when we rewrite our story in a way that leaves out its darker aspects, forcing ourselves to see the glass as half full. But it is just as impossible to be free when we are constantly berating ourselves for our sins and can only see the glass as half empty. Both of these mindsets show a similar lack of confidence in ourselves.

Self-confidence has to be a confidence in the *whole* of ourselves. The self is not a pure, unified, and perfectly coherent core on which to build and sustain our confidence. Such a core does not exist. Anyone who says we have to find it in order to have confidence in ourselves is lying to us. Worse, they are pointing us to a dead end. We only have to examine ourselves for a moment to realize this. Where would such a core be located? In our brains? Our stomachs? Our heels? Our genomes? The self is multiple, paradoxical, changing: it's when we are mindful of its complexity that we experience our freedom, and this realization can come with the feeling that a dam has burst. We are no longer dominated by just one part of ourselves that tyrannizes us from the inside. Nor are we in thrall to a truth that descends to us from the heavens, dictating to us from the outside. We are freed twice over. We finally trust ourselves.

It is no surprise that Emerson, the philosopher of self-confidence, greatly influenced Nietzsche, who heaped such scorn on the

Conscientious One. The author of *The Twilight of the Idols* even wrote that Emerson was his "sister soul." It is also pertinent that Emerson was an American. He wasn't raised in one of the countries of Old Europe, taking pride in his country's multimillennial past and sifting it for answers to the questions of his day. Instead, he came from a young nation, one that was discovered by accident, and one that valued the pioneer spirit, which is the very spirit of self-confidence. In the United States, submission to what Max Weber called "the authority of the eternal yesterday" is less prevalent than in Europe. The pioneer has the courage to listen to himself. In fact, he has no choice, often being the first on the scene.

In each of us, a war is raging between the spirit of the Conscientious One and the spirit of the pioneer. Each time we listen to ourselves, the spirit of the pioneer gets the upper hand. The less we blindly obey dogmas and traditions, the greater space we create for self-confidence.

"Trust thyself," said Emerson, "every heart vibrates to that iron string." Let us learn to hear that vibration, to detect it. Let us pay less attention to the noise around us, to the voices of those who insist that "it's extremely urgent," that "this is something we can't argue with," or that "it's always been this way." These voices will never be silent. Being confident is finding the strength to turn away from them and hear ourselves.

FOUR

Expose Yourself to Wonder

When beauty gives us confidence

There can be no very black melancholy to him who lives
in the midst of nature and has his senses still...
While I enjoy the friendship of the seasons I trust that
nothing can make life a burden to me.
—Henry David Thoreau

If we still doubt our capacity to listen to ourselves, let us consider
all the times we trust ourselves without even realizing it.

It's a simple experience, one that happens to us regularly. We
are on a walk in the countryside when we are suddenly struck by
the beauty of a rolling landscape. We become lost in contemplation of a strangely luminous sky. We come across a song on the
radio that moves us deeply. And we find it beautiful. We don't
say that we find it pleasing. We say, "That's beautiful," as though
everyone should find it beautiful.

What a great deal of self-confidence it takes to utter a general truth
of this kind! We are confident enough in our judgment that we

don't need to support it with arguments. We make our judgment freely and without consideration of criteria. It's beautiful, and that's it. It's not beautiful *because* of anything. It's beautiful because there's no because. Although we are always quick to doubt ourselves, this is a moment when we are free of doubt. Looking at beauty allows us to listen to ourselves.

I remember a particular summer evening. I was walking to a beach in Corsica, thinking about my life, which was getting away from me. I had doubts about nearly everything. I needed to tighten up on the reins, but being disorganized, I didn't know how to go about it. I had to make a decision, but I couldn't make up my mind. Suddenly, I saw the light on the surface of the sea, a silvery sparkling. The light dimmed as the evening came on, but it was as though its intensity doubled. Everything was suddenly more real, more present. The shimmering reflection, paradoxically, suggested eternity. Without a moment's doubt, I thought: That's beautiful.

"That's beautiful"—the statement is simple and speaks with an authority we aren't often able to muster. On so many other occasions—at work or at a family gathering—we lack the ability to be authoritative. We have ideas, but we don't dare introduce them into the conversation. When we have an aesthetic experience, prompted by a dazzling sky, a singer's voice, or the opening notes of a cantata, we discover that we are perfectly able to listen to ourselves. Each time we say that something is beautiful, paying attention to nothing but the feeling it inspires in us, we are learning all over again how to trust ourselves.

"The beautiful is always bizarre," said Charles Baudelaire. And it actually is strange: the aesthetic experience is never simply aesthetic. By making us more present to ourselves and to the world, it also has the power to awaken us, provoke us, and perhaps even strengthen our self-confidence.

Most likely our aesthetic sense has this power because it draws on the totality of our being. When I think that the Corsican landscape is beautiful, it isn't just my sensations that are called into play. Of course, my senses are a part of it, but my aesthetic pleasure cannot be reduced to a sensuous pleasure, to a stimulation of the eyes and ears. The landscape also reflects values and a sense of meaning. It makes me think of the infinite, of God, and of freedom. My pleasure has an intellectual dimension in addition to the sensuous one. I am conscious of liking this landscape, but it also fascinates me for reasons I'm unconscious of, awakening the most secret parts of my being. When we are open to beauty, we don't just listen to one part of ourselves, we respond to all our faculties in harmony: our sensations, our intellect, our unconscious, and our imagination. This harmony allows us to talk about confidence in ourselves, in our whole selves, and not simply confidence in our sensibility or our rational minds.

In his writings on the mystery of the aesthetic experience, Kant speaks of "the free and harmonious play of the human faculties." When the beauty of a landscape strikes us, the internal conflicts that so often wear us down seem to stop miraculously. We are no longer torn between our reason, which orders us to do this, and our emotions, which ask us to do that. The internal cacophony momentarily stops. We are finally in agreement with ourselves. Listening to ourselves then becomes much easier.

Looking at an artist's work, we are often tempted to ask ourselves "what did he mean by this?" That train of thought may then dominate and drive out the inner harmony of the kind we instinctively feel in front of a beautiful landscape. If we try too hard to figure out what the artist meant, we lose the opportunity to discover what his work makes us feel. At times, we react to a work of art in exactly the way that we react to a natural landscape, without asking ourselves about the intentions behind it. Looking at the work or listening to it is all we need, and it fills us with deep joy and makes us attentive to what is going on inside us. How many adolescents, filled with self-doubt, have discovered David Bowie or Tupac Shakur and gained a kind of self-assurance from listening to their music? They feel confidence in their own judgment: no question, this is beautiful. And how many men and women who normally find it hard to have confidence in themselves have suddenly felt authorized, when listening to Mozart's *Requiem* or Schubert's *Fantasia in F minor*, to listen to themselves? They don't need an expert to tell them what emotions Schubert has expressed musically in this masterpiece: dashed hopes, human arrogance confronting its limits, a sometimes sweet melancholy, and joy that surges brutally, in spite of everything. They need only let themselves be carried along by their emotions to know this. Exposing oneself to beauty, one comes closer to oneself. It is not simply an escape, but a plunge into the depths of oneself to find the possibility of confidence.

This is why we feel gratitude toward artists who bowl us over. We feel like thanking them for the power they give us. I discovered the novels of Françoise Sagan when I was about eighteen—the "little music" of her fluid writing, so deceptively simple. *Bonjour Tristesse*, which she wrote at the age of seventeen, starts with these melodious words: "In naming this unfamiliar feeling, both sweet and tiresome, that has lately been obsessing me, I hesitate to apply the grave and beautiful name of sadness." A writer is a voice, a held note. How is one to find that note if one doesn't know how to listen to oneself? Françoise Sagan was very young, but she was already able to do it. To continue to hold that note, she had to be able to hear the "little music" of her own words. The more I read of her books, the more I wanted to write. I told myself that I, too, could find my voice, my tonality, and that I could listen to myself with just as much freedom.

"Great works of art," Emerson wrote at the beginning of "Self-Reliance," "have no more affecting lesson for us than this. They teach us to abide by our spontaneous impression with good-humored inflexibility." In the end, when we say, "this is beautiful," we are speaking as much about the landscape or the song as we are about the confidence that is bubbling up in us, irresistibly. Each time that beauty touches us, it gives us the strength to dare to be ourselves.

The need to read criticism or to listen to audio guides or expert opinions in order to know whether something is beautiful, reflects a lack of confidence in oneself. When we give in to it, we reject our spontaneous feelings and accept a dictate telling us what to think—the very definition of snobbery. Once again, we are not trusting ourselves.

Let us expose ourselves to beauty, then, as freely and as often as possible. In the countryside and in the city, let us learn to open our eyes. Beauty is everywhere, and everywhere it engages with our freedom. Let us visit museums, but without giving ourselves over entirely to guides, only listening to them enough to boost our confidence. Let us not be too inhibited by our limited cultural knowledge, and let us dare to make the leap to direct and spontaneous interaction with artworks, the leap of self-confidence.

I remember the emotion I felt the first time I stood in front of a work by Mark Rothko. The canvas was enormous, yellow and orange. There it was, suddenly, right in front of me. A pure presence. Beauty is a presence that summons others to it. I stood in front of this Rothko the way I stood in front of the sea in Corsica, certain that it was beautiful, that there was something in this vibration of light, something eternal, something true—an extraordinary spiritual density at the heart of matter. Yet I knew nothing about it—I didn't even know who Rothko was. Still, I wasn't in any doubt. I had total confidence in my sensation, in my judgment, in me. It was all at once a confidence in this artist whom I didn't know, in art, in beauty, and in life.

Once we are able to welcome beauty readily, it can help free us from our inhibitions. Each time we recognize that something is beautiful without reference to external criteria, we are gaining confidence in ourselves. But beauty gives us more than that: it fills us with life force and helps us find our courage. We have all experienced this, in museums possibly, or while listening to music, or almost certainly when surrounded by nature. Beset with worries, gnawed by doubts, persuaded that we won't succeed, we set out walking in the countryside to look at snowy ridgetops or at the sunlight filtering through branches, and suddenly it seems that nothing is impossible.

It was something like this that I experienced in Corsica and that Henry David Thoreau, a close friend of Emerson's, describes in *Walden*: "There can be no very black melancholy to him who lives in the midst of nature and has his senses still. There was never yet such a storm but it was Aeolian music to a healthy and innocent ear.... While I enjoy the friendship of the seasons I trust that nothing can make life a burden to me."

Here the beauty of the seasons does more than authorize us to make a judgment. It fills us with aesthetic wonder, to the point of giving us the strength to believe in ourselves. It's actually hard to figure out what is happening here. What is it in the simple contemplation of nature that gives us confidence? After all, these beautiful forms are by definition superficial. So why do they affect us so profoundly, giving us the peace that fosters confidence?

Looking at nature may simply allow us to put things in relative perspective, to change the way we look. Before so much beauty, before the miracle of the dawning day, of this world taking shape under our eyes as though it were the first morning, we put a distance between our cares and ourselves. Before the mystery of this light, our worries suddenly carry less weight.

But there is something else. We sense that at the heart of beauty there is a force at work that is greater than ourselves, a force that we have confidence in. We are not looking at beauty that is external to us. Instead, we feel traversed by a power that is as much within us as without. At that point, we are no longer simple spectators of the world's beauty. We have been made aware of our own presence in the world. We had forgotten it, and now beauty has brought it back to our minds: we live in this world. It's not just something we have to make profitable or cost effective—it's our home. It is easier to have confidence in ourselves when we feel at home in the world.

"Why, then, do we prate of self-reliance?" Emerson asks. "To talk of reliance is a poor external way of speaking. Speak rather of that which relies, because it works and is." For Emerson, "that which relies" and "works and is" is a divine force whose presence we feel once we have moved away from agitation and rediscovered the peace of nature. What Emerson calls divine force, the Stoics call cosmic energy, the Christians call God, the Romantics call Nature, and Henri Bergson calls *élan vital*, or vital impetus—but the name hardly matters. Is this not exactly what we feel when we let ourselves become absorbed in contemplating the sky, or when we look at the gnarled stems of a grape vine and its cluster of ripe berries, or at sunflowers turning to face the sun throughout the day? Truly, something in the beauty of nature "works and is." We then come to understand that self-confidence can't simply be confidence in ourselves. It is also confidence in what is at work in nature, in the force that travels through it and pierces us with its beauty. We come again to the idea that self-confidence is always, in part, confidence in something other than ourselves. Just as a child finds self-confidence from knowing that she can count on others, the self-confidence we get from beauty is at the same time confidence in the force that vibrates in nature and makes it so beautiful.

Finally, when we look at nature, which has consoled so many men and women before us, when we say, "this is beautiful," we are also showing confidence in all people, in a possible agreement of all people on the subject of beauty. It's as though the harmony we feel within ourselves makes us want to be in harmony with all others. This harmony, this agreement, is likely not to happen, but in the moment of our emotion, we wish for it to. In the intensity of that second, we believe in it. "It's beautiful," says our faith, in a general invitation to partake. For this reason again, self-confidence is confidence in something other than ourselves: in beauty, in its power at work, but also in a possible agreement between all people, whatever their differences.

The rock climber Patrick Edlinger was an aesthete as much as he was an extreme sports athlete. Watching this man, who revolutionized climbing, make a free-solo ascent without any protection and climb the sheer walls of the highest mountains is truly fascinating. In the documentary that was made about him, *La vie au bout des doigts* (Life at one's fingertips), what first impresses the viewer is Edlinger's technical mastery, his pure competence, which appears all the more readily because he climbs without any equipment, wearing shorts and a T-shirt, and carrying a small bag of chalk at his belt. His gestures are so perfect that he seems to effortlessly change handholds, the weight of his body passing from one hand to the other. When he reaches behind to dip his free hand in the chalk bag, he is hanging over the void, held by nothing more than his other hand, specifically, the tips of his fingers. As we gradually learn about his way of life—he lived in a trailer deep in the most extraordinary landscape—and as we listen to him answer his interviewers, we start to understand that the contemplation of nature was central to his preparations. He lived, in the very real sense of the term, in the midst of this beauty, in communion with the forces of nature. When he wasn't training, either strengthening his muscles or increasing his flexibility, he was absorbed by the blue of the sky, the majesty of the summits, or the arrogant simplicity of the ridgeline, in an uninterrupted dialogue with the world's beauty. Where did he draw his confidence from when he started out alone, with no climbing partners or protection, on an extremely risky climb? Clearly, he relied on his abilities and his experience. But he also put his confidence in nature itself, in the beauty that gave him so much strength and accompanied him day after day. It is impossible to separate the confidence that his great skill gave him from the confidence that he drew from the world around him—from the natural elements, the very balance of the world, of which beauty is the index and perhaps even the proof.

His example is rich in lessons for us all, even if we don't make barehanded ascents of the world's highest summits.

It tells us that relying on ourselves to the maximum extent, by developing our talent as far as possible, does not keep us from counting on something greater than ourselves.

It tells us that behind self-confidence there is a less well-known confidence, a more secret but also a deeper one, in something other than oneself.

It tells us that we can let ourselves be inspired by beauty—it can be the best of guides.

FIVE

Decide

Confidence in the midst of doubt

In all things, the wise man looks not at the result
but at the decision he has taken.
—Seneca

When we change our minds endlessly and can't bring ourselves to
make a decision, we tend to blame it on a lack of information,
data, or knowledge. But we are speaking in bad faith; most often,
what we lack is confidence. As we have just seen with aesthetic
experience, when we decide that a particular landscape is "beautiful," it isn't because we have a store of irrefutable arguments to
support us, but because we dare to listen to and trust ourselves.

A young woman has received a job offer that appeals to her,
but she hesitates. The job she has now is not very stimulating,
but it offers her a degree of comfort: a decent salary, amiable colleagues, nearness to home, and job security. It is not her dream
job, but she's pretty happy with it.

The position she is being offered is the one she has been hoping for, and it comes with the prospect of finally developing her talent. But the company is a new start-up, located far from her home; she doesn't know her future colleagues; and the base salary would be slightly less than she is earning now. She could eventually earn more, but only if the business is successful. So she hesitates. On the one hand, there is security, a pleasant daily life, and no passionate engagement with her work but a certain tranquility, which is reassuring to this woman who is raising two children on her own. On the other hand, the new job would offer more scope for her ambition, but also more risk, for herself and her children. As soon as she starts to lean one way, she becomes paralyzed at the thought that she might be making a mistake. Time passes and she is still unable to decide. How is she to emerge from her irresolution? How will she find her way to a decision?

To decide is to find the strength to engage with uncertainty, to move forward surrounded by doubt, in spite of doubt. It is to make up for the lack of definitive arguments by using the ability to listen to yourself, or come to a decision simply to get moving again. In both cases, it's a question of having confidence in yourself. Committing yourself in that way is not easy: you have to shoulder your burdens and be ready to deal with unpredictable consequences. But that comes with the territory. Decisions oblige us to choose without having recourse to an ungainsayable argument. Not blindly, but without absolute clarity either.

This difficulty is an essential feature of life. Because we are free beings, because we are not machines running on a program, we have to accept an element of uncertainty. And we need to do more than accept it: we need to find a way to welcome it. This is what the young woman is unable to do. Every decision is by definition risky: the more we accept this element of risk, the more we will be able to make effective decisions and enjoy making them. Even if we reduce the risks as much as possible, some will always be left. If we are not able to accept that element of risk, we will not be able to come to a decision, or we will do so with fear in our bellies. And make poor decisions.

Our lives constantly force us to arbitrate between competing courses of action. We aren't sure whether it's the right moment to take a job, to move our household, or to change fields. But no one can make the decision for us, and it is incumbent on us to be up to the task when a decision is called for. If we don't fully assume our power to make decisions, our life will be a series of non-choices, and it will slip away between our fingers, taking our confidence with it. You can't have self-confidence without mastering the difficult art of making decisions.

Philosophy can be helpful here by pointing out the difference between choosing and deciding, which we often confuse. The two terms are sometimes used as synonyms. In fact, each has a different logic.

To choose is to choose logically, rationally, after an investigation that has reduced the element of uncertainty to practically nothing. Let's say we are considering two vacation destinations. If one has more objective advantages than the other and corresponds better to our expectations while costing the same amount of money, then we choose it. We don't need any real confidence in ourselves: all it takes is an ability to reason and calculate correctly. But when two destinations are both attractive for different reasons and there's no objective criterion for choosing one over the other, then we will have to decide.

To choose is to rely on rational criteria to support a course of action. To decide is to make up for the inadequacy of the criteria by making use of one's freedom. To choose is to know before acting. To decide is to act before knowing.

We are, therefore, freer when we decide than when we choose, because we are not obliged to go along with inarguable criteria. But this freedom is often unsettling to us.

In our example, the doubt that the young woman feels at times changes to anxiety. She is fearful of the consequences of her choice. If she doesn't move to the new company, she knows she will have to take responsibility for her humdrum but comfortable life, and that she won't offer a very inspiring example to her children. If she takes the risk of changing jobs, she knows she'll have to shoulder the risk of instability and expose her family to it as well. She would like not to have to decide. The truth is that her own freedom is what causes her anxiety.

———

In our professional lives, we often talk of decisions when it's really only a question of choices. If it's just a question of going along with common sense or the results of an Excel spreadsheet, if we just have to follow custom or the regular procedure, then, properly speaking, there is no decision involved. The question of decision arises when we have exhausted the resources of our reason and some element of uncertainty remains. If we can't be sure that our choice will be the right one, then we are faced with the prospect of having to make a decision—from the Latin *decidere*, "to cut off." It's precisely because we *don't know* that we have to decide! And it's hard to do. It would be so much easier if we could choose. We suffer because we would like to make a choice when life requires us to make a decision.

To live better, Ludwig Wittgenstein reminds us, it sometimes suffices simply to think better, to clarify a few conceptual distinctions. Understanding the difference between choosing and deciding can help us as much in little things, like ordering at a restaurant, as in big things, like changing jobs or committing to a relationship. When we are looking through the menu at the restaurant, if we wait until we are sure of not making a mistake in deciding between the roast chicken and the pork shoulder, we may wait a long time—and make our tablemates wait too. Only by accepting uncertainty will we manage to decide faster.

Why is the young woman unable to decide whether or not to accept the job offer? Because she tolerates uncertainty poorly. Consciously or unconsciously, she seems to be waiting for a data management application to analyze her case, draw a picture of her future, and spit out the correct option. An app of this kind does not exist. And that's what makes life beautiful. But she forgets that. We all tend to forget that. We are paralyzed by uncertainty because we forget how dull life would be if everything were certain and predictable. Of course, we can make mistakes. And of course, the consequences can be painful. But this element of uncertainty is the salt in our lives. If we deny the real fact of uncertainty, the denial will gnaw at us from inside and take our clarity of mind from us—and our ability to listen to ourselves. If, on the contrary, we accept it fully, we will paradoxically find the courage to make difficult decisions. Fortified by our lucidity, we will make our decision in good conscience. We will be able to accept more calmly the possibility, inherent in any decision, of opting for the wrong alternative.

Increasing our self-confidence requires an inner transformation: we must open ourselves deeply to the acceptance of uncertainty. This act of opening up is hard for us because we normally use our intelligence to limit our exposure to uncertainty. It's here that we need a philosophy, possibly even a traditional wisdom. "The sky is inside," says a Sri Lankan proverb, suggesting that many revolutions start with an inner transformation. There will always be uncertainty—this is a reality we can't change. But we can change our response to it. Denial is what exhausts us and causes us anguish. Everything is easier for the person who manages to stop denying and face uncertainty head-on.

In the end, that's what happened to the young woman in question. She was jogging along the banks of the Seine, in Paris, finding her rhythm, feeling good. She suddenly saw uncertainty differently: "Success is not a given," she told herself. "The future is not written anywhere. That's the way things are. But I'm going to take a stab at it. I've decided: I'm changing jobs." She was fully aware when she made her decision. She felt strong. Not because she was sure of having made the right decision. But simply because she had decided.

This acceptance of uncertainty is the first step in our inner transformation, in acquiring the wisdom to decide. But acceptance can turn into active consent and change into a special form of pleasure, perhaps even joy. We may in fact reach the stage where we like the idea that our decision may not be the right one. Because the possibility of being wrong reminds us that we had the courage to make a risky decision and that life is not an exact science. The more we consent to the possibility of error, the more we experience ourselves as free beings, capable of acting decisively. To have confidence in oneself is to learn to love one's freedom, rather than to be afraid of it. There is a special joy in knowing that one is capable of it.

In *Western philosophy*, the thinker who has drawn the difference between choosing and deciding with the greatest clarity is Søren Kierkegaard. The author of *Either/Or* uses this distinction to define his own faith. He sees his faith as a "meta-rational" leap, a leap beyond the scope of reason, of rational choice. In other words, a pure decision. He mocks those who claim to "choose" God, bringing faith down to a question of theological arguments, values, or, worse yet, rational demonstrations. In his view, these people lack confidence both in God and in themselves. They are not free. For a mystic like Kierkegaard, it is pure madness to believe in God: a beautiful madness perhaps, but madness all the same. He might have subscribed to Blaise Pascal's remark that "there is no proof of God, only the experience of God." We have no "reason" to believe in God. If we look at the record of violence in human history, at the imagination men have shown in perpetrating evil, the preponderance of reasons would lead us not to believe in God. But that, says Kierkegaard, is why we are truly free to believe, to decide that God exists. If God's existence could be established by scientific reasoning, by a system of equations or by pointing to the intricate workings of the world, then there would be no need for belief: his existence would belong to the field of knowledge. But if nothing proves his existence, if we cannot point to any objective argument, then we can only rely on ourselves for our belief. By saying that faith is based on a decision and not on a choice, Kierkegaard frees it from its entanglement with dogmas and arguments—it becomes a question for the free heart, for pure confidence. He also tells us something essential: the farther a decision is from being supported by a simple rational choice, the more it requires that we have confidence in ourselves.

This confidence in ourselves, when it reaches a certain critical point, joins with a confidence in something other than ourselves. Self-confidence, for Kierkegaard the believer, is at the same time faith in God. But it could also be faith in the future, in others, or in life.

To decide is to take a stand at the heart of uncertainty, at the heart of life itself. Each time we consciously make a decision, we learn how to trust ourselves a bit more.

The little issues that we meet in daily life can therefore provide us with opportunities to train. They can be seen as a kind of practice run, a preparation for the big decisions. Let's train ourselves to make decisions more quickly, while accepting our own uncertainty, not denying it. We are standing in front of our mirror in the morning: pants or a dress? This little top or this shirt? Do these jeans look good on me? The question arises, but need it take so much time to be settled? We arrive at our desk, where a Post-it note lists the things we have to do. Where do we start? As simple as it might seem, we arrive at self-confidence by training ourselves in this way: learning to decide more quickly about little things. Each time, we learn to trust our freedom a little more. If we can't come down on one side or the other in the little things, how are we going to manage when the stakes are higher? The better we become at deciding, the more we will have confidence in ourselves, and the more this confidence will also nurture our ability to decide, in a kind of virtuous circle. On the other hand, the less we are able to decide, the harder it seems to find the strength to do it. At some point, life will make the decisions for us. "There is no problem that an absence of solutions will not eventually resolve," the French politician Henri Queuille once joked. Not deciding is a kind of decision in itself, but the poorest and least affirming kind.

The ability to decide is something that should be taught more in schools. There's no lack of opportunity for instruction. In high school, to take just one example, many teachers who give their students the "choice" between a number of different essay subjects could point out that the main purpose of the exercise is to learn to make a decision, and to make it rapidly. They could tell their students, "It's not because a topic is good that you select it. It becomes good because you've selected it, because you've chosen to put yourself behind it." They would be helping their students who lack self-confidence and spend too much time "choosing" their subject, weighing the pluses and minuses at great length, as though a surefire reason for opting for one topic or another were suddenly going to emerge.

How is it possible that, even today, a "decider" on subjects of political or economic moment may have studied at a succession of elite schools without ever taking a single course on decision making? Such courses exist in various political science institutes, but they are optional. In business schools, courses on decision making have appeared in recent years, but often under the title "science of decisions," which seems to confuse the subject with the logic of making choices. "Art of decision making" would be more accurate.

Let us teach our children early on the difference between choosing and deciding. Let's tell them they mustn't wait until they've eradicated every last doubt in order to make a decision. Their freedom lies in being able to move forward with a decision while doubt remains. Let's remind them that the heroes who have carried humankind forward committed themselves without being sure of the outcome—Gandhi, Charles de Gaulle, Martin Luther King—all had the courage to confront uncertainty. Let us teach our children that they have this power, this sovereign right in uncertain circumstances. We can make them understand this even in very simple situations. They are hesitating between two gifts, two workshops, two friends to invite home. We can tell them straight out, "Go ahead, jump in, make a decision. You won't have more elements to work with tomorrow or even in ten minutes. And most importantly, if you don't make the decision, someone will make it for you. What do you prefer? In any case, even if you make a mistake, life will have taught you something. Have confidence in yourself, have confidence in life."

Each time we make a decision, we can see that self-confidence is at the same time confidence in life. If we make a mistake, we can always adjust our aim. "The voyage of the best ship," said Ralph Waldo Emerson, "is a zigzag line of a hundred tacks." The ship has no other choice when the wind comes at it directly but to bear off a bit: it must tack back and forth to make headway upwind. We are like this ship, forced to advance crabwise, to try things and then make adjustments. "To err is human," says the proverb. This doesn't just mean that we should have compassion for those who make mistakes, but that making wrong choices is the human way of learning. Making a bad decision, then correcting for it—this is not just one way of proceeding among many others—it's our only avenue for moving forward. Being the human animals that we are, the wind is always in our faces.

Deciding always takes you out of your comfort zone. In our lives, our jobs, our daily dealings, and our relationships with others, there are fortunately many things that we do not have to decide. We often have enough facts on hand simply to choose, and we are sufficiently in control that we don't have to take the risk of deciding. We can rely on customary practices, on general know-how, and on certainties. The whole trick is not to allow this logic of control, of choice, to swallow up our capacity to decide, our ability to enter the zone of "uncontrol" and make the leap at the heart of every decision. Instead, it should nourish that capacity to decide, motivate it, and give it a solid base.

We reassure ourselves, then we take risks. We know how to choose, then we have the courage to decide. Self-confidence is, we've said it before, a two-time waltz.

SIX

Getting Your Hands Dirty

Doing to develop confidence

Matter exists for him. It is stone, slate, wood, copper....
The true engraver starts on a work in a daydream of volition.
He is a worker. He is an artisan. He has all the glory of the laborer.
—Gaston Bachelard

Here is the story of a brilliant intellectual, Matthew B. Crawford,
who holds a doctorate in philosophy and who worked as executive director of a Washington think tank. In a fascinating book,
Shop Class as Soulcraft, he describes how thoroughly depressing
he found his office work, even starting to doubt his own value
and usefulness, and how he recovered his confidence by quitting
and opening a motorcycle repair shop!

Crawford shows how easily we can lose confidence in ourselves when we spend our days in an office and have no precise grasp of what we are doing or the effects of our actions.
Conversely, he shows us how manual work, the fact of working
with our hands and modifying the real world with our actions,
can have a liberating effect, both emotionally and intellectually.

Using humor and sharply drawn observation, he compares the satisfactions provided by his two successive occupations, offering a striking case for manual labor generally and a mechanic's job in particular. He convincingly shows that the manual labor he performs has its mental element, and that it is in fact more nourishing intellectually than many less physical jobs. Based on his own experience, he revisits the experience of those who work to make or repair things—jobs that are disappearing in a world where we simply buy, throw out, and replace. He talks of the pleasure he feels at immersing his hands in crankshaft oil and doing something tangible. He describes the direct responsibility he feels when a motorcycle's owner puts the machine in his hands, and his satisfaction when he overcomes the difficulty of making the repair. He feels confidence in himself, and a shared joy when the owner comes to collect his motorcycle. This is the happiness of what he calls his "face-to-face" with the client.

"A man is relieved and gay," wrote Emerson, "when he has put his heart into his work and done his best; but what he has said and done otherwise shall give him no peace." Surprisingly, motorcycle repair gave Crawford, an intellectual, the opportunity to "put his heart into his work" and "do his best." He hadn't been able to do this before. At his important post in an influential think tank, he'd spent his time juggling political sensitivities and political footballs. His work consisted in reading and synthesizing academic articles, interpreting them to align with the ideological tenor of the think tank that paid his salary. If his experience was particular, he nonetheless experienced a form of alienation that is familiar to many of us: executing tasks that make no sense. He also encountered another common problem:

because he had to churn out his syntheses at a rapid rate, he couldn't read the scholarly articles in depth, and he produced shoddy work that he derived no pleasure from.

By contrast, when he is repairing motorcycles, he takes pleasure in spending time on a breakdown that resists his efforts, truly grappling with it, and deepening his ability. He feels again what he felt at the age of fourteen when he worked as an apprentice electrician: the pleasure of doing something concrete and seeing the results. He tells how he never got tired, when he'd finished a wiring job, of turning on the switch and saying: "And there was light!" We've all had that experience. We have just finished fixing a shelf, or repairing a piece of furniture, or adding a coat of paint and we exclaim, filled with a joy that exceeds our small accomplishment: "That's work well done!"

In our work lives, we too often lack the opportunity to rejoice in this way; we are cut off from this joy.

Crawford contrasts his own joyful rediscovery of manual labor with the dominant ideology of his times: "The flitting disposition is pressed upon workers from above by the current generation of management revolutionaries, for whom the ethic of craftsmanship is actually something to be rooted out from the workforce.... The preferred role model is the management consultant, who swoops in and out and whose very pride lies in his lack of any particular expertise. Like the ideal consumer, the management consultant presents an example of soaring freedom, in light of which the manual trades appear cramped and paltry: the plumber with his butt crack, peering under the sink."

What Crawford says rings all the truer given that the reality experienced by the new generation of managers rarely conforms to this picture of "soaring freedom." A large number of management consultants and other corporate types who never peer under a sink suffer from not knowing what it is exactly that they do, what purpose it actually serves. Their lack of self-confidence therefore has a very simple explanation: in the face of criticism, they have no concrete and objective reality to point to. A baker can always argue to his boss that he does good work—the freshly baked and delicious loaf is there, and you need only taste it to agree. Artisans have an easier time being confident—their talent is expressed objectively and tangibly in the objects they make—and they often earn a better living than office workers. We've all met those slightly gruff plumbers and electricians. They aren't looking for compliments or for anyone to express a liking for them. The leak has been fixed, the light has come back on—that's all they need.

Reading Crawford's book, we understand better what our problem is today. We make fewer and fewer things, both in our professional lives and at home. When our car breaks down, we drop it off at the garage. Even the mechanic spends more time looking at a computer screen than tightening bolts. Soon we won't even have to drive our car to the garage, since cars will drive themselves. When our telephone or our laptop computer stops working, repair programs launch automatically. And when the updates no longer solve the problem, we toss the thing away and buy a new one. When we are looking for warmth, we are now in the habit of regulating the thermostat. We no longer perform those activities that, not so long ago, were part of a person's daily routine: cutting and splitting logs, stacking firewood, setting fireplaces, keeping a fire going. When we are trying to find our way, we no longer open a map and ask passersby to help us; instead, we follow orders from our GPS. We are losing our direct relationship with things. Thanks to our super-connected digital devices, we are increasingly disconnected from the world of making. Our thumbs glide over the surface of our smartphones, and we glide over the surface of things. "The civilized man has built a coach," said Emerson, "but has lost the use of his feet. He is supported on crutches, but lacks so much support of muscle." It's hard to have confidence in yourself when you can no longer walk. Think how panicked we get when our iPhones don't work. Without our digital crutches, we can no longer get around. When we neglect the fact that we have a body, we lose the sensuous relation to the world that is so central to confidence. James Baldwin, who as it happens was influenced by Emerson, wrote well about sensuality and the risk we run of losing confidence in ourselves when we ignore our body and our senses: "The word 'sensual' is not intended to bring to mind quivering dusky maidens or priapic black studs. I am referring to something much simpler and much less fanciful. To be sensual, I think, is to respect and rejoice in the force of life, of life itself, and to be *present* in all that one does, from the effort of loving to the breaking of bread." To be "present" in what we do, there is nothing "simpler" or more down to earth than to roll up one's sleeves and get one's hands dirty. Baldwin, who lived an expatriate life in France after World War II and returned to the United States in the 1950s, pursues this train of thought with seemingly ironic comments on the quality of bread in the United States, but his irony is quickly replaced by an earnest reflection on confidence: "It will be a great day for America, incidentally, when we begin to eat bread again, instead of the blasphemous and tasteless foam rubber that we have substituted for it. And I am not being frivolous now, either. Something very sinister happens to the people of a country when they begin to distrust their own reactions as deeply as they do here, and become as joyless as they have become.... The person who distrusts himself has no touchstone for reality—for this touchstone can be only oneself." For Baldwin, it's impossible to have self-confidence when you are so cut off from your body and your senses that you're not even aware of what you're putting in your mouth. This diatribe, written in the middle of the last century, resonates particularly today in the age of industrially raised animals. How can we have confidence in ourselves when we seem to have lost touch with even our most basic senses? The indifference that Americans showed to the "tasteless foam rubber" they called bread struck Baldwin as a symptom of the crisis of confidence that Americans were then experiencing. In making his case against a white America that is incapable of even the most basic sensuality, Baldwin shows that "whatever white people do not know about Negroes" (notably their experience of racism and their strength in still embracing the joys and heartbreaks of life despite that racism), "reveals, precisely and inexorably, what they do not know about themselves."

When he was recently asked about the most important changes that have occurred in our time, the French philosopher Michel Serres unhesitatingly answered that it was the disappearance of traditional rural life. It has meant not only the disappearance of the men and women who worked the land but of their world, which was a world where the people made things and knew what they were making, where they related sensually to their bodies and to material things. The world where, once their work was done, people could see the fruit of their labor. Their pride and their identity came from the tangible evidence of their work, and when life dealt them a harsh blow, that visible presence gave them back a little of their lost confidence.

The cabinetmaker who builds a table out of wood knows what he is making. The baker who kneads her dough and bakes her bread does too. Both take all the more pleasure in their task when they do it well and derive all the more joy when they improve. Both feel a sense of satisfaction in giving pleasure to their clients, who return to them because they recognize their talent.

This simplicity, this direct and immediate recognition of our work is what we are most cut off from. At the office, we "work with our hands" less and less and spend more time in meetings, or looking at our computers, or dealing with emails and filling out spreadsheets. We work to achieve goals that rarely have any direct bearing on the quality of the finished product. It is not uncommon for us never to see the finished product, or to particularly care. Consequently, we don't see ourselves reflected in our work. We are evaluated on whether we achieve intermediate goals set by managers. We have to respect protocols, check the work of our subordinates, and report to our superiors. It is hard in this context to say just what our profession is. When at night an artisan tells his child about his work, the child understands what his father has spent the day doing. By contrast, many children of corporate executives don't understand what their parents do for a living. Once when I was giving a philosophy workshop in a first grade class, a seven-year-old girl told me: "My mom's work is going to meetings."

So what does the idea of "good work" mean here? Can we still talk about "expertise"? Where can we find pride if we no longer know what we do? How can we have confidence in our talent if we don't know what that talent is? Work-related stress and the increase in burnout and depression are largely due to the disappearance of traditional occupations. As process and striving for intermediate goals become all-important, the yardstick for success becomes money. But the compensation is largely illusory. The sense that you're not making anything tangible can't be erased by higher pay and the opportunity for greater consumption. If it did, there wouldn't be such a high rate of burnout among well-paid white-collar workers.

Self-confidence is the child of pleasure: the pleasure we take in doing something well. If we no longer "do" anything concrete, if our professions are not really professions at all, if they don't allow us to develop a true expertise, then we find ourselves deprived of the elementary pleasure of doing and making, alienated from ourselves and without self-confidence.

The workplace is experiencing a twofold crisis. Workers and employees are under the permanent threat of being replaced by machines; and managers are fixated on process, which deprives them of their freedom and alienates them from their trade. Burnout and loss of confidence flourish on this cultural substrate.

———

A *good occupation*, according to Aristotle, should provide pleasure to the man or woman who follows it, and the excellence of that person should be directly observable to others. In a society that values "the good life," he said, we should all have an occupation, or a trade, that meets these criteria.

In his *Economic and Philosophic Manuscripts of 1844*, Karl Marx defines the ideal of work in this way: "In my production I would have objectified my individuality, its specific character, and therefore enjoyed not only an individual manifestation of my life during the activity, but also when looking at the object I would have the individual pleasure of knowing my personality to be objective, visible to the senses and hence a power beyond all doubt." Let us be attentive to the terms used by the author of *Capital*: "objectified my individuality," "enjoyed an individual manifestation of my life," "the individual pleasure of knowing my personality to be objective." These evocative terms are so many metaphors for self-confidence. How many of us are lucky enough to have occupations that give us that?

The fact that we lack a direct relationship with making, that we have a hard time recognizing ourselves in the product of our labor, surely contributes to our anxiety. Making something, even if it is something extremely simple, more often than not is enough to rid us of this anxiety. Just the fact of rolling up our sleeves and working with our hands, never mind the result, is enough to boost our confidence. There is a surprise twist here. It is that our anxiety is always, to a more or less secret degree, anxiety about death. But in working with physical material, we are in contact with a reality that we can count on, something tangible and reassuring. The transformed material proves in and of itself that we are alive and, if it is nicely transformed, that we have talent. Furthermore, if our work gives us a confirmation of our value, we can more easily endure the prospect of death, since our value, at least, will not die. When we do nothing, or when we get no direct recognition from our work, we are more immediately susceptible to our anxiety about death.

"It is not because he has hands that man is the most intelligent of beings," writes Aristotle in *On the Parts of Animals,* "but because he is the most intelligent of beings that he has hands. Truly, the most intelligent being is the one that is capable of making skillful use of the greatest number of tools; and the hand would seem to be not a single tool but several." Crawford has put into practice what Aristotle discovered twenty-four centuries earlier. To be intelligent is to use one's hands! To use them intelligently. The hand is the extension of the rational mind. This simple statement is of vast significance. If our intelligence is extended by our hands, then it is logical that not using our hands will cause us to feel doubt about ourselves. We lose confidence in ourselves as a result of not making anything with our hands—we are cut off from our true selves, from our nature as *Homo faber.*

Our nature, as Henri Bergson has argued, is more nearly that of *Homo faber* than it is of *Homo sapiens.* Our *Homo sapiens* ancestor was more of a maker (*faber*) than a knower (*sapiens*). What distinguished humans was not so much their wisdom as their ability to fashion tools and make things using those tools. Our intelligence is not primarily an abstract intelligence but a fabricating intelligence. *Homo faber* is the human who works with intelligent hands and who makes and uses tools. When we make things, we make ourselves. The different ages of human existence are named with respect to the tools that shaped us and allowed us to make progress (Stone Age, Bronze Age, and so on). We are made to construct, manipulate, work, and experience our faculties in contact with the world, and alter matter to develop ourselves and our talent. It's in relation to matter that our mind reveals its true nature. That is why we feel lost, strangers to ourselves, when we no longer make anything with our ten fingers. The renewal of interest in cooking, in do-it-yourself projects, and in all the other manual activities has deep roots.

In recent years, a sizable number of young business school graduates and corporate executives have turned toward artisanal work. They complete a certificate program to become bakers, pastry chefs, or cabinetmakers and set off on a new adventure. Giving up one's attaché case to open a restaurant or abandoning a career as an executive to make cheeses is no longer so unusual.

And though we needn't go as far as changing our lives, nothing stops us from working with our hands a little more than we do. Painting and making pottery, working in the garden or around the house, these are all opportunities to rediscover the joy of making, of doing things well. To make things with your hands, your intelligence, and your heart: this is the road to a sturdy self-confidence.

SEVEN

Swing into Action

Acting to gain confidence

The secret of action is to start in on it.
—Alain

A young man is preparing for a night of love. He is nervous. It's his first time. The woman lying at his side has made a deep impression on him. He has been dreaming of her for a long time, and he imagines that she must be experienced. The time is now. But he himself has no experience. Where then will his confidence come from? From action, first of all. From very real caresses and kisses. This reality is something he is holding, cupped in his hand, pressed against his lips. It's by starting to enter into the game of caresses, then by making love, that he will really gain confidence in himself. And not before! His confidence comes from his relationship with the woman beside him, from the bond that he has woven with her. If he pretends to be a man of experience, he runs the risk of being shut inside himself, of finding no support in his relationship and being unable to perform. If, however, he admits that it's his first time, he can let himself be guided by her: his confidence will come from her. And though coming from her, it will become his. This is the natural process by which self-confidence arises: a gradual appropriation that action alone makes possible. I'd so like to have known it at the time.

How many virginal young men make a botch of their first time because they are obsessed with performance, caught up in their interior monologue, and counting solely on themselves to make it happen! Failure is their punishment for not having had enough confidence in their relationship and for not having given themselves over to it enough, in the present moment. Failure is their punishment for having located their confidence in the "self." When we act in the world, we are not alone. And if there's one realm where we truly need to remember this, it's in the realm of sex. In our sexual lives more than anywhere else, only action liberates us.

Psychologists, teachers, coaches, athletes, and theoreticians of positive psychology all agree in saying that self-confidence develops through action. But a misunderstanding often slips in behind that generally agreed notion. While self-confidence may be gained through action, it is not a pure confidence in "self," separate from the world, as though we were monads with essential qualities needing to be developed in action. It is a confidence in the encounter between oneself and the world. An encounter that we do not entirely control, which will hold surprises for us and be rich in lessons learned. Through action, we discover new opportunities in the real world and unsuspected resources that our action helps uncover. As our action brings us in contact with others, the solution may come from them, or in the end prove simpler than we imagined, or we could even have a stroke of luck! You need to have confidence not just in your "self," but in the encounter between yourself and others, between yourself and the world—which only taking action can set in motion.

This nuance is decisive, and it can be liberating. When I am paralyzed by a lack of confidence, the fact that I need to "go for it" may strike me as a paradoxical instruction. Maybe taking action will help me gain confidence, but how, if I lack self-confidence, do I gear myself up to act? I may feel less weighed down and find the impetus to act if I understand that I have to have confidence not just in myself but also in the encounter between the world and me, and in the consequences that will flow from that encounter. These will sometimes be lucky, sometimes less so, and often unexpected.

Defending a philosophy of confidence inevitably brings up the first principle of Stoic wisdom: not everything is dependent on us. There are things that depend on us and things that don't. The Stoic worldview, from Marcus Aurelius to Seneca, is founded on this distinction. We must act, of course, as much as possible on the things that depend on us, but being self-confident means that we must also have confidence in the things that don't depend on us and that our actions may set in motion. Often when we lack confidence and when we put too much pressure on ourselves, it's our understanding of the world that's at fault. We have forgotten the Stoics' insight and assume that everything depends on us. There is no surer way of "botching" one's first time.

Let us take inspiration from men and women of action—adventurers, pioneers, entrepreneurs. Even when they have spent a long time thinking before they start, they have confidence in action itself and in all that it sets in motion in the real world, directly or indirectly. They know that their action will have the power to reconfigure the world around them, create new opportunities that they will have to seize. Even if they make every effort to control the things that depend on them, they know how much does not depend on them, which may emerge as a hindrance or help. They are ready. Though they may have drawn up a detailed course for themselves or a fine-grained business plan, they know that action in and of itself will modify the parameters. They may need to alter their route to avoid a storm or take advantage of better-than-expected weather conditions. They may have to launch a new product that will correct the flaws of the first, or they may have to double down on the first one they launched. They have to stay attuned to how others and the world around them react. That is the true spirit of enterprise: to have the ability to predict and enjoy doing it, but also to embrace all that remains unpredictable.

From outside, many entrepreneurs and adventurers seem to be carved from a solid block of confidence. Up close, it turns out that many of them don't hide their doubts or past failures. But they have confidence in action, in all that can happen once an encounter with the world occurs. They know, just as Marcus Aurelius did, that the outcome of the encounter doesn't depend solely on them. And they are not in any way resigned to this inevitability; instead, they welcome it.

I've often noticed that entrepreneurial men and women like to play the go-between, even when they have no direct interest in the outcome, just because they think that a particular matchup could be interesting, make something happen. They like to bet on what's still uncertain, to start something going that may have a bright future. They know, as all bold people do, that luck can be provoked.

A young executive asks for a meeting with her boss to increase the scope of her responsibilities; a young filmmaker knocks on the door of a director he admires to show him his work; these men and women who have the courage to take the first step—let's not mistake their boldness. If they take action, it's not necessarily because they have confidence in "themselves" before taking action. More than anything, they have confidence in action itself.

Before she became one of the most widely read novelists of her time and won more than fifty literary prizes, Isabel Allende grew up in Chile where, the moment she mentioned her ambition, people told her it was impossible because she was a girl. Yes, she might be the niece of President Allende, but she was still a girl. She grew up in a man's world with a strong sense of that world's unfairness and without a single female example to inspire her. As a young journalist, she was assigned to interview the poet Pablo

Neruda, and she had the audacity not to stick to the prepared questions. She gave free rein to her spontaneous inspiration. Neruda, she says, interrupted her with these words: "Look, you lie all the time, you make things up, you put things in people's mouths that they haven't said. These are faults in journalism, but they are virtues in literature. So you'd do better, young lady, to devote yourself to writing fiction." She might never have become a novelist had it not been for this encounter. And yet, she hesitated about whether to conduct the interview at all. She didn't feel legitimate. So she didn't go into the interview with any great feeling of confidence. Yet it's because she went ahead with it that she found her freedom. It was during the interview that she gained confidence. Actors who suffer from stage fright have the same experience time after time: they become confident when they go onstage—not before.

If we fail, or if we are less successful than we'd hoped, at least we will have succeeded in trying. Every day among my students I see how an inability to try leads gradually to a loss of confidence. I sometimes invite them to get up and speak, in a more or less impromptu mode, on a very difficult subject. Those who make a stab at it gradually gain confidence in themselves, even if they don't fully overcome the difficulties of the exercise. To the other students, they seem like the ones who have tried, who have made a start. This is already something to be proud of. By trying, they have found that they are capable of new ideas, of intuitions they hadn't expected. They don't need to be successful at the exercise in order to draw satisfaction from it. On the other hand, those who continue to hang back never gain self-confidence. By not going for it, not grappling with the real world, they never get the chance to find the thing that might free them from being blocked. They fall into a vicious circle: by not taking action, they deprive themselves of action's liberating qualities, and their anxiety does nothing but grow.

When we understand the benefits of action, we are no longer tempted to define it as the simple outcome of thought. We are the product of centuries of Platonism and Western rationalism, which have valued the work of the intellect and the contemplative mind over direct action; hence our difficulty in recognizing the primary power of action. It's true that thought must often precede action, but it doesn't follow that action is of less value than thought. Otherwise, we'd never be able to find the confidence we need when it comes time to act: we'd continue to tremble each time our thought failed to dispel every uncertainty, which it will never do. Action is never a question of putting into practice a project that has been thoroughly planned. It is the encounter of a person with no great confidence in himself or herself and a world that is only partly predictable. The truth of action can therefore not be found in the thinking that precedes it: it can only reside in the action itself. "The secret of action," as the French philosopher Alain said more than once, "is to start in on it!"

Let's not forget that in order to survive on this earth in the midst of the dangers that threaten us, we humans have had to act and react since the dawn of time. We are more the product of these millions of years of evolution than of the few centuries of Platonism. We sense this when we take our courage in both hands and force ourselves to make an opening remark to a person we are interested in or to stand up to speak in public. Just the fact of going into action awakens our primitive self with its primordial combativeness, which plays so important a role in our confidence.

Too often, the psychologists, teachers, and coaches who stress the importance of action as a means of developing our self-confidence don't put enough emphasis on the idea of action as an encounter with the world, with others, and with reality. Action is too closely associated with one's will as a simple means of testing one's abilities or developing one's skills. It is sometimes seen as nothing more than a training ground for strengthening one's will. But to act is to do more than to train; it is to come in contact with the world. There's nothing to say that the world won't be kinder to us than we expect. To act is to give oneself the chance of being pleasantly surprised, the chance to experience the world's kindness.

In presenting self-confidence as a philosophy of action, I am proposing an existentialist, not an essentialist, view of it. From the essentialist's perspective, having confidence in myself comes down to believing in an essential "me," an indivisible core deep inside myself, an unchanging and all-important ego. Such an idea, spouted in video after video about self-confidence on You-Tube, is problematic.

There is no evidence that such an essence of the self exists, that we contain such an essential and fixed "being." If there is a point on which Freudian psychoanalysis, contemporary philosophy, the neurosciences, and positive psychology agree, it is that personal identity is multiple, plural, and changing. This is something that should reassure all the people who suffer from lack of self-confidence: the fixed and immutable "me" does not exist! Also, we can't "be" nothing, since what we "are" is in flux. Most often, our lapses in confidence originate in childhood traumas: we were underappreciated, publicly humiliated, treated as essentially mediocre. The classic philosophic distinction between being and becoming can in such cases be liberating. We *are* not: we are in the process of *becoming*. We don't have confidence in ourselves? It doesn't matter. Let's have confidence in what we are capable of becoming.

Seeing confidence in one's "self" as confidence in one's essential being or deep nature also runs the risk of causing us to bypass much of the beauty of life.

Our lives are fascinating not because they allow us to unpack gradually the abilities of a me in which everything is already contained at the outset, but because they give us the chance to invent ourselves and reinvent ourselves, to rebound from setbacks and embark on new courses, to discover unexpected potential within ourselves. And it's a good thing too, or we wouldn't be free. If life simply consisted of unfolding the possibilities of an essential self, then "essence" would in fact precede "existence." But in Sartre's formulation, "existence precedes essence," meaning that before all else, we exist. Our confidence has to be placed in that existence, not in some hypothetical essence, which for Sartre only takes shape on the day we die, when we can no longer add anything to our story.

To exist is to take the plunge, to go forward toward others and the world, toward the obstacles that we can turn into opportunities, as long as we are willing to change how we see things. So many things can happen once we get ourselves moving, and we can put so many forces into play once we are engaged, and meet so many men and women who can help us, voluntarily or involuntarily, that even the expression "confidence in oneself" sounds beside the point.

To act is to invite the self to take part in the swirl of existence, to step outside itself rather than persist in thinking it encompasses the pure essence of its value, to "burst" outward rather than huddle in on itself. This is the meaning of the title of one of Sartre's main works: *The Transcendence of the Ego*. The ego's value is "transcendent" in that it operates and is operated on outside the ego, through its capacity to act, to forge relations with others, and to take part in the dance of life.

Going into action can be understood to apply to an individual, but it can also apply to a group. The existentialist model of self-confidence provides a good way to see how collective action can restore confidence to individuals who are suffering from oppression, trying to assert their rights, or struggling for recognition. "Stepping outside of oneself" then, means entering into a collective with others, forming a group capable of fighting, advocating for itself, and boosting its members' confidence. Here again, individuals will find their confidence restored only after taking action and through taking action, not before. If you were born in the wrong neighborhood or on the wrong side of the tracks, if all your life you've been excluded, humiliated, and dominated socially to the point of feeling the invisibility that Ralph Ellison named and described in *Invisible Man*, his masterpiece on the condition of black people in America, then it won't do you much good to be told you have a sparkling jewel inside you, a magnificent essence you can have confidence in. An invitation to reclaim your rights, your dignity, and your freedom through collective action will likely prove more useful. At that stage, having confidence in yourself as an isolated individual will not be enough. You will have to develop confidence in a collective self, a collective "we."

Don't have confidence in yourself, then. Instead, have confidence in what your activity is able to create in order to provide you a point of contact with the world and with others. Have confidence in what depends on you, and confidence also in what doesn't. Have confidence in the reality that your active presence is already busy transforming. Have confidence in the luck that your actions can stir up. Have confidence in the men and women that you will meet and who will maybe give you ideas, advice, hope, strength, and—why not?—love.

EIGHT

Admire

Confidence and exemplarity

I could never read a philosopher whose life was not exemplary.
—Nietzsche

She was twenty-eight years old when her first novel, *Indiana*, appeared in 1832. Written in a month and a half, it was praised by Honoré de Balzac and François-René de Chateaubriand, who were soon joined by Victor Hugo and Alfred de Musset. Aurore Dupin, writing under the pen name George Sand, made a spectacular entry into the literary world. Even the most merciless critic of the period, Charles-Augustin Sainte-Beuve, conceded her talent after reading her second novel, *Valentine*, which appeared a few months after the first. He even compared George Sand to the brilliant early nineteenth-century writer Madame de Staël. Beginning with her first novel, George Sand defended a woman's right to act according to her passions and urged freedom from domestic oppression. She expressed her boldness not only in her novels, through their style and subject, but also in her private life. To satisfy her desire to write and her belief in freedom, she courageously asked her husband, a young and un-objectionable baron with whom she had had two children, for a divorce. She had nothing against him except that she found him boring, that there was no complicity between them, and that he was entirely ignorant of literature. To understand just what a decision of this type must have cost, we need to re-create the context. At the time, divorce was illegal, and George Sand's property, including the beautiful family estate she had inherited at Nohant, became the property of her husband, Baron Dudevant, starting on the day she married him. But George Sand fought determinedly. After a long lawsuit, she managed to divorce the baron and keep the house at Nohant, where she would entertain many writers, painters, and politicians. In the meantime, she lived in Paris with her lover Jules Sandeau, half of whose name she took to become "George Sand." Traveling between countries and also between men (she counted as her lovers some of the great figures of the century—the poet Alfred de Musset; Frédéric Chopin, with whom she lived for nine years; the engraver Alexandre Manceau; the writer Prosper Mérimée; and perhaps a few women as well), she always supported herself by her work and absolutely refused to be kept by anyone. A pioneer of today's feminist movement, she rejected being called a "woman writer" and asked to be judged solely on the merits of her work.

On the political scene, Sand showed the same force of char-acter. She became a republican after 1830, and then a social-ist. She championed poetry for the working classes. She started writing more politically engaged novels that dealt with current social issues, and she was as successful with these as she had been with her earlier feminist novels that featured inspiring heroines, including Indiana, Fadette, and Consuelo. Just the fact that she was willing to take a new tack in changing literary genres is proof of her self-confidence. A prolific author, she also wrote short stories and plays, meeting with critical and popular success throughout her life.

When she learned that the *Revue des deux mondes*, a literary monthly, considered her articles too radical, she straightaway started her own magazine, the aptly named *Revue indépendante*, with the philosopher Pierre Leroux. A militant journalist, she also started a newspaper, *La Cause du peuple* (The people's cause), which had a second life when it was revived by Jean-Paul Sartre in 1968. And to crown it all, George Sand was fully invested in her role as a mother. Her children's happiness was of great concern to her, and she admitted to a heartfelt "passion for her progeny," which she was able to reconcile with her love of literature and her passion for freedom.

George Sand lived a full life, one that exuded confidence at every level; she had an extraordinary capacity to "go for it," to continually make daring decisions, to keep creating. On what, an observer can't help asking, did such an abundance of confidence feed?

When we look at her biography, we learn that her early life was chaotic. Her father died in an accident when she was only four years old, and her grandmother took her almost illiterate mother to court for the right to raise her. The grandmother was awarded custody. A product of the Age of Enlightenment and a rich and cultivated woman in her own right, Sand's grandmother made a persuasive case that she was better suited to raise a child than her daughter-in-law, a young and penniless widow with little education. Consequently, at the age of four, little Aurore lost her father and was taken from her mother, who accepted a monthly stipend in exchange. For all intents and purposes, Aurore was bought from her mother by her grandmother—not an obvious way to develop an unshakable confidence in life. True, the girl would grow up in the care of her progressive grandmother, tutored by a humanist scholar, and in the natural surroundings of the Nohant estate, ensconced in a forest that she learned to explore on horseback. Not a negligible start in life, but it doesn't explain how she became such a bold, free woman, able to go out into the world with such confidence and courage.

Aurore Dupin became George Sand, by her own account, because she was a great admirer. At every stage of her life, she admired unusual personalities, people who had the courage to become themselves. It was through these inspiring examples that she found the strength to impose herself, as though her fascination with the talents of others allowed her to take hold of her own talent. The whole history of her life confirms that the admiration of others gave her wings.

As a child, Aurore Dupin had unbounded admiration for her great-grandmother, a woman whom she had never met but who had a high profile in the eighteenth century: Louise Dupin. Aurore constantly asked her grandmother for stories about her and devoured any writings in which she appeared. Louise Dupin, who has been called "the feminist of Chenonceau," held one of the most highly regarded literary salons of the Age of Enlightenment. She was a friend of Jean-Jacques Rousseau, who fell in love with her, and she made her mark on the era by her freedom of thought and her passion for literature and philosophy. Rousseau was convinced that she would have earned a place in the history of ideas had she published the essays on which she was working. "The mind deliberates, and the heart decides," she wrote, which is a good definition of self-confidence and the art of decision-making. So Aurore Dupin grew up admiring this erudite woman who was ahead of her time and who gathered in her salon the greatest minds of the eighteenth century.

Then, as a young woman, George Sand admired Marie Dorval, a popular actress who revolutionized the classical theater with her Romantic style of acting, which was both passionate and sensitive. George Sand expressed her admiration for Dorval in an open letter, in such strong terms that the two were thought to be lovers, though that was probably not the case. It is easy to see the traits in Marie Dorval that inspired George Sand, the same traits that had inspired her great-grandmother, such as freedom, boldness, the willingness to break with tradition, the commitment to feminism, and the marriage of mind and heart.

An accomplished writer, George Sand also admired Gustave Flaubert, with whom she kept up a long correspondence and whom she twice hosted at Nohant. She was dazzled by the genius of his novel *Madame Bovary*, then by the evocative power of *Salammbo*, his next novel. And she admired Flaubert's reinvention of himself in moving from one to the other. When *Salammbo*, an orientalist tale, was panned by the public, George Sand came to his defense, writing to him in a letter: "Nothing is more ill-suited to indulge the mental habits of the social set, the superficial, and the hasty [...], which is to say the majority of readers, than the subject of *Salammbo*. The man who conceived and executed this project has all the aspirations and fervor of a great artist."

But the person she admired most and who became her true mentor was the socialist philosopher Pierre Leroux. Propounding a "religious socialism" in which Christian charity would prevail in human society, he embodied a form of humanism that was both pragmatic and idealistic. She admired his belief in progress, his reasoned criticism of private property, and his feminism. Leroux was all in favor of the civil and social equality of the sexes, and a supporter of women's suffrage. Highly critical of the institution of marriage, he was also an apostle of nonviolence.

We could easily add to the list of those whom George Sand admired, each time gaining a better understanding of the personalities that marked her intellectual progress. In identifying with one after another, she built her own identity and found the strength to invent herself. Among those she admired were free women, writers who moved from one literary genre to another, thinkers committed to social causes, and many others. They had all the characteristics that she developed gradually in herself but in her own way, following her own path.

The kind of admiration we are talking about here is not the fascination that fans have for their idols, but a fertile admiration, a deep curiosity about the life of a person who succeeds in becoming his or her true self—a keen enough interest in the talent of another that it can tell us something about the possibilities of our own talent.

To admire is not the same as to venerate; it doesn't mean losing oneself in the contemplation of another's talent. It means nourishing oneself, following the example of those who've had the courage to follow their star, and undertaking to find one's own. What does their example tell us? That it's possible to become oneself.

We always doubt the possibility. And we have every reason to do so. Convention, social norms, established procedures all exert enormous pressure on us to conform. It's so much easier not to break ranks, not to make waves.

Freud demonstrates this masterfully in *Civilization and Its Discontents*: societies rest on the individual's renunciation of his or her singularity. If there is to be society, then there must also be behavioral norms. The upshot is "discontent," since the individual is well aware that the norm must prevail over individuality. It's therefore natural for us to experience sudden losses in confidence, even to the point where we may sometimes ask ourselves whether it is thinkable that we might someday become ourselves. When doubts overtake us, what we need is proof— not from rational argument, but from example—that it's always possible to find our way. Admirable examples are always more effective, more freeing, than grandiloquent speeches. Admiration can save us from a loss of confidence: if a thing was possible once, then it must be possible now.

Admiring as she did her great-grandmother, "the feminist of Chenonceau," George Sand knew that a woman of letters could
make a place for herself in the world of men. She saw it was
possible. Admiring Flaubert as she did, she knew that a writer
could have the courage to pursue his quest and reinvent himself,
even at the risk of losing readers. If she ever started to doubt it,
if she was ever tempted to reproduce the same recipe over and
over again, she would only need to remember her admiration for
Flaubert, and she would find the strength she needed to resist
the mounting tide of inner fear.

To admire is always to admire the idiosyncratic. That's how
admiration differs from respect: everyone deserves respect, but
we admire those who have had the courage to become themselves. And since what we admire about a person is his or her id-
iosyncrasy, it would be absurd to copy it. We admire this person
for being inimitable. And the inimitability is what inspires us.

George Sand didn't imitate Flaubert when she wrote. Her
style is different, as are her themes and motivating obsessions.
But George Sand's admiration for Flaubert made her a better
writer. She drew inspiration from the way Flaubert became Flaubert in order to become George Sand.

When she welcomes Prosper Mérimée, or Eugène Delacroix,
or Prince Napoléon to her Nohant estate, she doesn't imitate
her great-grandmother hosting a literary salon at Chenonceau;
she doesn't copy her, she draws nourishment from her. She finds
inspiration in the way Madame Dupin became Madame Dupin
to become George Sand.

A great role model becomes an example for the very reason that the person can't be copied, according to Nietzsche. A

great man gives those who admire him a dream of greatness; exemplariness is like a bridge that spans the space between one idiosyncratic person and another. Alexander the Great inspired Napoleon because Napoleon, being unable to imitate him, had no choice but to become Napoleon. Similarly, the artist's desire to create a masterpiece comes from the recognition that the great marvels of past geniuses cannot be imitated. The more clearly George Sand understood that Marie Dorval, Flaubert, and Pierre Leroux were inimitable, the closer she came to her own star.

"Become what you are," says Nietzsche's Zarathustra. But to do so, admire those who've managed it for themselves. Admire and then admire some more. Admire more than one person, and each will sustain you and help you move forward. Every time you admire, you are seeing the radiance of an idiosyncratic star. Each time, you are seeing the possible radiance of the star that is your own.

Nietzsche too was a great admirer. He admired the philosopher Arthur Schopenhauer, but also the composers Richard Wagner and Franz Liszt. Pablo Picasso didn't hide his admiration for Diego Velázquez, Francisco de Goya, and Édouard Manet. Madonna admired David Bowie, Tamara de Lempicka, and Frida Kahlo. The French writer Philippe Djian has spoken of his debt to Henry Miller, Richard Brautigan, and Raymond Carver. Yannick Noah, the tennis star, admired his own father, and Arthur Ashe, and Mike Tyson. Ralph Ellison might not have written *Invisible Man*, which won the National Book Award in 1953, had he not admired Richard Wright and his major autobiographical work, *Black Boy*, published in 1945. In a review titled "Richard Wright's Blues," Ellison wrote, "Nowhere in America today is there social or political action based upon the solid realities of Negro life depicted in *Black Boy*." This admiration, which also extended to Dostoyevsky, Mark Twain, and James Joyce, would not keep Ellison (whose full name, Ralph Waldo Ellison, was given to him by his father, in tribute to none other than Ralph Waldo Emerson!) from launching into his own writing project no more than a few days after reading *Black Boy*.

These names speak for themselves; to take someone as an example is to make a start. To admire is to come out of oneself, the better to come back to oneself eventually.

Today, we no longer admire enough. We give our attention to messages or people who "create a buzz" on social media, taking up the space previously held by men and women who had spent years developing their talent, finding their idiosyncratic path, and acquiring fame. Since the arrival of reality television in the late 1990s, we've seen the headlines of our media outlets and the guest lists of our talk shows fill with ordinary men and women, people who are demonstrably average, selected not for any particular talent but because they lack any particular talent, so that the greatest number may identify with them. Showcasing so many people without admirable qualities is an unprecedented event in the history of mankind. It could be an occasion for self-confidence—at least these "models" are not too intimidating. But it works in just the opposite way. It's disastrous to have no one to admire.

When we relax by watching a popular entertainment show, when we surf social media for such and such a star of reality television, when we allow ourselves to be swept up by the shallow buzz that one of them has created, we often assume an ironic stance. This is a way of reassuring ourselves. By mocking them, we remind ourselves that we are giving our attention to people without merit, but that we are doing so knowingly. We are allowing ourselves to have a moment of rest and relaxation.

But this irony is an illusory protection. We think we're not being duped, but that's exactly how we are being duped. Because we think we're immune, we agree to waste our attention and let ourselves be contaminated by a worthless exhibition. That is precisely the meaning of the title of a workshop given by Jacques Lacan: "The non-dupes are duping themselves." Thinking we have not been duped is the surest way of entering into complicity with the things that diminish us. We may not have been duped, but while we looked on ironically, all those minutes, those hours, have been stolen from us. While we look on ironically, we are not admiring anything. Admiration is always a direct emotion.

"*Become what you are*"—and you have to do it before you die. Our time is short. And instead of admiring people whose example elevates us and makes us want to believe in ourselves, we walk towards our deaths paying attention to nonevents and enriching those who've scripted them. The irony that is so pervasive nowadays puts everything on the same level and prevents us from admiring anything. It flattens things out, whereas admiration makes distinctions. There is something morbid in the triumph of irony, in the loss of enthusiasm.

———

"*Give me work, exhaustion, pain, and enthusiasm!*" says Consuelo in *The Countess of Rudolstadt*, George Sand's masterpiece. The little bohemian was to become a great singer simply because of her voice, her courage, and her admiration for Maestro Porpora. There's no irony on Consuelo's part—she is too alive for that.

NINE

Stay True to Your Desire

The antidote to a crisis of confidence

> The only thing you can be guilty of is
> to have given up on your desire.
> —Jacques Lacan

These days, we have innumerable ways to compare ourselves to others. It is the worst poison for self-confidence. On Facebook or on Instagram, there are always people who, at least in appearance, are better looking than we, richer, more cultured, better connected, more committed—whose lives are better than ours. Previous generations never had the same problem; they couldn't inflict damage on themselves so easily. They couldn't sit on their sofas and watch the parade of images displaying the success and happiness of others. They compared themselves only to those they were close to. Those they didn't know remained unknown to them, and all their distant acquaintances and the celebrities were cut off from them. Comparisons could only be made within one's group, between individuals who were mostly part of the same world. Everything is different today. We measure ourselves across social milieus, across the country and the world: an inexhaustible source of frustration. And the worst is that we make our comparisons based on elements that are often stage-managed, and therefore potentially deceptive. No wonder we lose out, time and again. The comparison tells us that we aren't any good, but without telling us how to get better. It hurts us without giving us insight.

On social media, we don't compare two realities according to fixed and objective criteria. We compare our own reality—which we know and do not confuse with our self-presentation—with what others show of themselves. We may be well aware that the pictures of people's lives posted on Facebook and Instagram have been labored over, retouched, and carefully selected, but they are still "real" to us, and we can't help comparing them to our own real life. Generally, it's a kind of attack, a diffuse but unrelenting source of narcissistic wounds. We have all heard of those It Girls whose thousands of followers attend to every detail of their enviable lives, although the girls' lives are in fact anything but enviable, to the point that some of them commit suicide. Yet we can't help crediting what we see with our eyes. It is the same thing with the photographs of models in illustrated magazines. We know the pictures are retouched, but we still compare the models' bodies to our own imperfect ones. We are bombarded with images that tell us more or less implicitly that we travel less, earn less money, live in less beautiful places, and consort with less interesting people—that, in a word, our lives are less accomplished than those of our "friends" and those we "follow," at a greater or lesser distance. They are only pictures, of course, but we see them every day and they have an element of truth. It takes only a moment of weariness or some passing difficulty for them to overwhelm us.

This poison is also harmful in that it can reawaken wounds suffered in childhood that undermine our self-confidence—the impression that our parents loved another sibling more, or the feeling of having been dropped by the object of our affections for someone else, or the shame of having been at the bottom of our class. In France, school is all about rankings. Every student's classroom work is returned in front of everyone. The poison of comparisons is administered from a very young age. It convinces children that their value is measured against others and not themselves, and that satisfaction is to be found in surpassing others, not in perfecting oneself. In all these scenes from childhood, the cause of our suffering is comparison.

The fact of comparing ourselves turns us away from the truth of our lives—we are all idiosyncratic. Our value is absolute, and not relative to the value of others. We are, each of us, alone in being what we all are: solitaire diamonds. We can compare some of our social achievements, but the particular brilliance of a solitaire diamond cannot be compared, by definition, with any other. By just being aware of our distinctness, we undercut even the idea of comparison. In the end, you can only compare things that resemble each other, but no distinct singularity resembles any other. Simply put, no comparison between two individuals is valid.

"*We but half express ourselves*, and are ashamed of that divine idea that each of us represents," wrote Emerson. For him, to become your singular being is to give life to the divine element that you harbor within you and that resembles nothing but itself. Any comparison with others is therefore doubly absurd; the same divine nature courses through us all, and each of us brings it to life in an individual way.

Nietzsche, although a ferocious atheist, acknowledged Emerson's influence in developing his philosophy of the individual. He divided individuals into two kinds.

On the one hand are those who live a diminished life, who feel guilty for being alive, and who are slaves to the dominant morality and to behavioral norms. They are constantly comparing themselves to others—they want to know who obeys best, who conforms most completely. Their disease of always comparing is the flip side of their obsession with norms.

On the other hand are those who dare to truly live, who have the courage to affirm their individuality, express their strongest desires. They wouldn't conceive of comparing themselves to others. They measure themselves by their own standard of measurement, by what they were yesterday, or a week, or a month, or a year ago. Have they made progress? Have they betrayed themselves or, on the contrary, have they come closer to their individual star? Have they become a little more what they are? That is the only question that matters. It's enough for them to chalk up some progress, even a tiny amount, to gain a modicum of confidence. And it's a form of confidence that is much less subject to erosion from a comparison with others.

Nietzsche's superman, often misunderstood, does not define himself in relation to others but in relation to himself. He wants more nearly to become himself, not to surpass others. He tests his limits. He lives intensely, takes a passionate interest in anything that might increase his life power. He doesn't equate the increase of his own power with the lessening of the power of others. He only compares moments, the degrees of intensity with which he is able to say "Yes" to life, to *his* life. The stronger that "Yes," the more alive he is, and the happier. Nietzsche drives this point home: the superman is a possibility that exists in each of us. We sense this when we take a passionate interest in an art form or some other kind of activity, when we refine our talent, when we feel that we have found a path in life that corresponds to our nature. The joy we feel in developing our abilities dispels any idea of making comparisons.

Joy is "the passage from a lesser to a greater perfection," according to Spinoza. We experience this every day, and we see it in children. When the joy of such an "increase" fills us, it vaccinates us at the same time against the virus of envy and protects us against resentment. Living our passion in the present moment absorbs us entirely. Sorrow, by contrast, is, in Spinoza's words, "the passage from a greater to a lesser perfection." It's when our power is diminished that the temptation to make comparisons beckons us.

———

To resist this temptation, to avoid the ravages of envy and jealousy, you need to know yourself well.

If I know what I aspire to, where I am, and where I am going, I won't compare myself to people who aspire to something else. And I won't feel myself in competition with people who start at a different point and work toward different goals than I do.

But if I am not very clear about who I am, if I don't know where my desire lies, then all the desires of everyone else become my desires. The risk I then face is of losing my footing, now that the field of competition has grown immeasurably vast, and of becoming riddled with envy.

If I know myself well enough to realize that my deep desire is to pursue the calling that is mine—an intellectually satisfying one that perhaps is not very well paid but that offers me a good quality of life—why would I be jealous of a person who makes lots of money? If my desire is to deepen my relationship with the person I love, why would I be jealous of a friend's flitting from relationship to relationship? Of course, I'll keep comparing myself to others. That can't be helped, belonging as I do to a social species. But this comparison, from the moment I am faithful to my desire, won't be painful, won't affect my desire, and won't really affect me.

"The only thing you can be guilty of [...] is to have given up on your desire," said Jacques Lacan in his *The Ethic of Psychoanalysis.* Not

giving up on our desire and remaining faithful to it, is to remain over our center of gravity. It doesn't mean being faithful to our essence or our identity, but to our quest, to a way of being and living that corresponds to us and is in large part inherited from our personal history. When we are unfaithful to our desire, we feel guilty—cut off from ourselves, from what really counts for us. When we are cut off from our truth, and floating, we are much more likely to compare ourselves to others and to be jealous of them. How can we then have confidence in ourselves?

We can have no real self-confidence unless we are faithful to ourselves, unless we have internal coherence and the deep joy that accompanies that coherence. Faithfulness to our desire is the antidote to the corrosive poison of comparison.

Many cases of midlife depression are caused by unfaithfulness to our desire. Men and women find themselves on the analyst's couch with no idea of what is making them unhappy. There is no "objective" reason. They have not lost someone close to them or been through a divorce. They are not having problems with their career. Sometimes they can even be quite successful, racking up one triumph after another. But they have given up on the crucial thing: their desire. In other words, they have been unfaithful to themselves. The function of depression is to help them hear what they have wanted to suppress. Depression makes them stop *wanting* in order to make a space for their true desire—to leave the comfort of apparent success in order to learn to know themselves again and to regain confidence in themselves by finding the path of their truth, their quest.

Ulysses made a long voyage, but he stayed faithful to himself, and that was the source of his happiness. He sometimes succumbed to temptation but was never entirely deflected from his course. In the roster of Greek heroes, he stands for the man who knows himself. That's why he asks his shipmates to tie him to the mast. He knows that he is drawn to the charms of the sirens. That's part of what a hero is: a man who knows himself, is aware of his strengths and weaknesses. He knows that he is curious, an explorer of the soul. But more than anything, he wants to return to his wife, his son, his hometown. The road home is a long one, from Troy to Ithaca. At every island where the ships make landfall there is a new world, inhabited sometimes by beautiful nymphs, sometimes by horrible monsters. Ulysses could easily take a wrong turn, for instance, by accepting the immortality that Calypso offers him. If he didn't know on a deep level what he wanted, he might compare his life as a mortal with the immortal life he is offered and start to envy it. He might also quake at the dangers he faces, be afraid he won't be able to surmount them. But something reassures him and supports him at the same time—he knows who he is, knows his desire. We can all draw inspiration from Ulysses's wisdom: He has confidence in himself because he has confidence in his desire. He knows himself enough to recognize, in the midst of all the stars twinkling like so many temptations, the one star that sparkles more than the rest, the one that shines for him.

TEN

Trust the Mystery

Confidence in life

Anyone who has seen a small child burst out laughing
has seen everything of this life.
—Christian Bobin

Confidence in life is both obvious and hard to define. We have already come across it several times in the course of our reflections,
but without exactly specifying its nature. To have confidence in
life is to bet on the future, to believe in the creative power of action, and to embrace uncertainty rather than being afraid of it. It
can be all of that at once, but it is also more than that.

It is to believe that there is something in life, in all life, that is
good, maybe even loving. It's to continue to love life even when
it seems hard. It's thinking that life doesn't need to be perfect to
be worth living. In its simplest form, having confidence in life
is to think that life is a good thing overall. To believe that deep
within the world, despite the ugliness that sometimes surfaces,
there is tenderness, a light that all of us have glimpsed and can

121

never forget. We don't really need to know where it comes from. We don't always know what we have confidence in when we have confidence in life. We have confidence, that's all: a confidence that has no object, pure confidence.

During the trials that await us, facing the difficulties we will encounter, in the depths of the darkest nights, we can warm ourselves at the memory of this flame. To have confidence in life is to have confidence in this glow, even when it weakens. We can have confidence in life because it doesn't go out, as long as we are still alive. Our trust in it will keep us from being knocked down at the slightest disillusion, and we won't lose our taste for life though it has disappointed us. Trusting it will allow us to have a more creative relationship with our abilities, as we will more readily venture out of our comfort zone and go toward others.

While self-confidence comes from competence, and while it is built on our relationships with others, the necessary medium for its existence, its nurturing soil, is confidence in life.

The Greek sages, whether Stoics or Epicureans, did not see "life" the way Jesus and the Christians would later come to see it. Nor does life have the same meaning for a vitalist philosopher like Bergson, or for a mystic like Etty Hillesum. It has a different meaning again for philosophers like Husserl and Maurice Merleau-Ponty, for whom living comes down primarily to inhabiting the world. According to our particular sensibility, we will find ourselves choosing sides with one or another. But all of these figures talk to us about having confidence in life. All of them tell us that to have confidence in oneself comes down in one way or another to having confidence in life.

According to the Stoics, life is a good thing because it courses with cosmic energy. The cosmos is a closed world, rational and divine, at whose heart we live. Try as we may, we can never deflect the course of fate. If we focus our efforts to coincide with the direction of fate's movements, we will be carried along with the current, and our actions will be amplified, crowning us with triumph. But if our actions run counter to the movement of fate, we will soon enough discover the powers that rule the world, even as we experience failure. For the Stoics, as we can see, the cosmos is in the end fairly benign: either it carries us along or it instructs us. How can we not have confidence in life? We live in a harmonious cosmos, and each of our actions puts us in contact with this harmony. For the Stoics, having confidence in life is having confidence in fate.

To the Epicureans as well, life is intrinsically good, but for the opposite reason from that of the Stoics. According to Epicurus and Lucretius, who were physicists as well as philosophers, everything that happens is contingent—reality is made of atoms that have met by chance. Everything that is could just as well not be: our bodies, the water we drink, the beauty of the world. Beings have no reason to be! The simple fact that a being has coalesced is a miracle in itself. It is a miracle that things exist, and my own individual existence is also a miracle. I, too, might not have been, and yet I am! Having confidence in life, for the Epicureans, is having confidence in chance, in the infinite scope of the field of possibilities. Atoms can combine and recombine endlessly to compose material things and living bodies. How can I not believe in life when it has given me the chance to exist, although my life was in no way foreordained? And what a wonderful way to keep things in perspective! We worry less about the chance of failure when we take into account the extraordinary victory of being alive at all. Furthermore, the elementary particles that compose us are eternal. We will die as individuals, but those particles will be reconstituted as other bodies. They will never stop celebrating the union of life and chance. Contemporary astrophysicists confirm the intuitions of the early atomists: we are composed of stardust—of electrons and neutrons that emerged from the Big Bang and that will survive us—giving material reality to the feelings of eternity that we sometimes experience. The life that inhabits us is vastly larger than we are. It was born more than thirteen billion years ago and won't end with us.

To Christians as well, the life that beats within us is larger than ourselves. Life is good, being the will of God. Have confidence, Jesus tells us, because everything is already here: love is not in heaven but deep in your own hearts. This confidence is more than a hope: you have only to believe in it, and the kingdom of God is at hand. That is the power of confidence, which has the same Latin root—*fides*—as faith.

———

"*Whoever has seen* a small child burst into laughter has seen every-thing of life," wrote the contemporary French author Christian Bobin in *L'épuisement* (Exhaustion). His poetry points us to the presence of God in the simplest things: a child's laughter, wrin-kles on a face, the flight of a dragonfly, a robin's breast. To a Christian mystic like Christian Bobin, Jesus's brief passage on earth transfigured the world, and nothing has been the same since. "The scents of flowers are words from another world," he says in *Les ruines du ciel* (The ruins of heaven). This other world is the kingdom of God, which is our kingdom also, but which we don't know how to see. The aim of poetry is to sensitize us again to this loveliest of worlds, which carries a trace of the original Love. How can we not have confidence when even the most prosaic things bear a trace of Jesus's passage? From this mystical perspective, confidence in life borders on surrender—the oppo-site of mastery. To have confidence in life is to surrender to its mystery.

"*We lie in the lap* of immense intelligence," said Emerson, "which makes us receivers of its truth and organs of its activity. When we discern justice, when we discern truth, we do nothing by our-selves, but allow a passage to its beams." Like Christian Bobin, he holds that to have confidence is to allow the beams of this "immense intelligence" to pass through us. When we think we are discerning truth or justice using only our human faculties, we are in fact letting God enlighten us. Emerson goes so far as to say, "we do nothing by ourselves." How better to express the idea that self-confidence can't be considered simply a question of mastery, given that an element of surrender always enters into it. This is something we can all understand, even if we don't believe in God.

Life, according to the philosopher Henri Bergson, is infused neither with cosmic energy nor with the love of God but with the *élan vital,* the vital impetus, a kind of primordial creativity that runs through all living things and is responsible both for the continuity of different species and the development of individual beings. Life is good because it is a pure force of change, of transformation. This life force is manifest in the growth of plants and the ability of ivy to make its way around obstacles, in the cunning of the fox and the speed of the horse, and in our practical intelligence and the creative genius of our greatest artists. In each case, it is the same *élan vital,* but in a different form. To have confidence in life is to have confidence in the creative force that wants to express itself through us, finding obstacles just a pretext to show its full powers. "Joy," writes Bergson in *Creative Evolution,* "is always the announcement that life has succeeded, that it has gained ground, that it has notched a victory: every great joy has a triumphal note." We do feel joy when we manage to wrench ourselves from acting automatically and are creative—that's when we feel truly alive. This upwelling of joy tells us that we not only have confidence in ourselves but in the creative power of life itself: it is this power that overflows in our joy.

———

And confidence in life can, finally, take the form of confidence in the world. According to Husserl, we have no choice but to believe in this world. To be put into this world is to be invited to have confidence in it, or else no human life would be possible. On the day of our birth, we were *entrusted* to the world. To have confidence in life is also to have faith in the world, and to consider that confidence, and not distrust, comes first. Without confidence of this kind, which Husserl qualifies as "original" and "a universal ground," we would feel we were living in a hostile, foreign universe. Madness would infect us. A primary belief in the world is not a decision, rather it is the condition for all our future decisions, our future trust, and our future distrust as well. How can we have confidence in ourselves if we don't have at least the minimum of confidence in a world that is real and where we have our place?

This helps us better understand why the contemplation of nature does us so much good: it reminds us that we are at home in the world, our world. Some artists know how to depict this original feeling, and they move us for this reason. Merleau-Ponty believed Paul Cézanne was one of these artists, for instance, when he painted the different versions of Sainte-Victoire Mountain. In the painter's brushwork, Merleau-Ponty sees the shimmering of the world at the moment when it first reveals itself to us, first resolves into the world. And Cézanne's mountain does not look to us like an object at a great distance but one that is caught in the same fabric as ourselves, part of the same flesh of the world, showing the same original confusion between the world and us. That's why ecological issues are so important: to take care of the world is also to take care of ourselves. Having confidence in life, for Husserl and Merleau-Ponty, is having confidence in a world that is not separate from us but of the same flesh. The world does not belong to us. We belong to the world. For that reason, it's natural to venture out into it.

For all that the Stoics spoke about the cosmos as ultimate rationality, they were forever dazzled by the mystery of its existence. The Epicureans may have developed a materialist approach based on atoms, but their whole philosophy is a meditation on the mystery of the contingent, and therefore on life. Christians, for their part, openly embrace mystery and are all the more convincing when they do so—as in the works of Søren Kierkegaard and Christian Bobin—rather than when they betray mystery by claiming to elucidate it, which makes faith a matter of dogmas and values. The Bergsonian *élan vital* is just as mysterious, being a spiritual force that endows matter with life. And mysterious also is the "flesh of the world" that Merleau-Ponty describes and that he calls the subject of Cézanne's art and the first truth of the world: there is nothing behind it, nothing in front of or beyond it, but everything is there, in its palpable thickness, offered to our perception.

All these schools of thought recognize the mystery inherent in life. To think that confidence simply depends on mastery would be to turn away from this mystery, to avoid looking at it head-on. No solid confidence can be built on an avoidance of this kind. True confidence certainly requires that we have a mastery of some kind, but it also requires that we be able to surrender to what is beyond us, what is bigger than us—what we call, for want of a better term, cosmos, God, or life.

This is the paradoxical lesson to be taken from our trip through the history of the philosophies of life: to have confidence in ourselves is to learn to rub up against the mystery of life, to welcome it to the point that contact with it warms us.

We are a long way from the usual metaphors that life coaches turn to, particularly the more uninspired among them. Their analogies tend to draw on computer science or classical mechanics, in which there is much talk of "reprogramming," of "finding your user's manual," of taking a hard look at your "software," when it's not a question of the "combination to the safe." Anyone who makes an Internet search for "self-confidence" will immediately stumble across this kind of metaphor, alongside the "seven techniques to develop self-assurance" and the "three keys to confidence." Besides these metaphors, the search will turn up methods that rely on pure autosuggestion, along the lines of the Coué method: "Rise every morning and tell yourself that things are better today than they were yesterday," "Look yourself in the mirror when you get up and tell yourself you are a genius," "State your goals loudly and clearly," and so on.

These instructions are both stupid and unhelpful—stupid because they deny the complexity of the human spirit, and unhelpful because they are likely to increase our sense of guilt when we suffer from anxiety. If I lack self-confidence and someone tells me that it's easy to acquire it, that all I need to do is "reprogram" myself in seven days and motivate myself every morning in front of my mirror, how am I going to feel if it doesn't work? Am I not going to feel even more responsible, even more at fault? I am struck by the brutality of these instructions, their lack of compassion.

Our habits are not like bits of twisted metal that we just need to untwist with a dose of motivation. We are not machines. Our thoughts are not defective programs that need to be rebooted. We are not computers. We are not going to blossom into our full potential just by saying positive things while standing tall in front of mirrors and breathing deeply. It's not with self-persuasion or self-manipulation that we are going to free ourselves from what holds us back.

There is no user's manual for a human life. In fact, that's why we're free and can choose the meaning of our existence. And even if our truth were tucked inside a safe, it would take more than a "combination" to uncover it: it would take time, a great deal of attention, patience, love, and that precious capacity to not try to understand everything, but to relax into the mystery of life.

One of the reasons for our lack of self-confidence is that life is hard and full of uncertainty. We will not shake off our fear of life by running from it and pursuing a fantasy of reprogramming our neurons or looking for our "personal user's manual" but by finding a way to live with our fear and lessen the threat of what frightens us. Life is living up to its reputation when it veers from what we expect of it—whether for good or ill. If it corresponded to our expectations, it wouldn't be life but a program executing its preplanned course—and we couldn't trust it.

Our discussion has already touched on the transformation of competence into confidence, the leap by which simple mastery can turn into true freedom and boldness. Only confidence in life can make this leap possible.

This was confirmed to me in an unexpected way during a lecture I gave on an airplane carrier, the Charles de Gaulle, at the Toulon naval base. I was speaking to a dozen officers of the French fleet's flagship and their commanding officer, Marc-Antoine de Saint-Germain.

My lecture was about confidence, and I was happy to share my ideas with the officers but slightly nervous at the same time. I suddenly wondered whether the notion of a self-confidence based on confidence in the mystery of life was one of those concepts that philosophers cook up and that prove inadequate in the face of facts. To explain to these military men who were soon redeploying to combat ISIS that their confidence should draw strength from the mystery of life suddenly seemed foolhardy, not to say absurd.

Intimidated by my audience, I found myself almost a child again, asking awestruck questions of his heroes. Their answers fascinated me, particularly those of two pilots of the Dassault Rafale fighter jet, who gave me a detailed account of night landings on an airplane carrier. And they explained the crucial role of the landing signal officer (LSO). During a night landing, the pilot cannot trust his instruments or his visual cues from the aircraft carrier—when he can see anything at all. He has to trust the spoken instructions radioed to him by the LSO, who stands on the carrier's deck. The LSO guides the pilot by voice in lining up the aircraft on the runway's axis for his approach pattern. The pilot has to surrender to the orders of the LSO. Even if he sees something, he can't trust his own eyes but has to follow his comrade's instructions with blind confidence. The pilot's self-confidence comes not only from his own highly developed mastery of piloting, but also from the absolute confidence he has in his LSO. What we find here, closely interlinked, are two major components of self-confidence: the technical component and the relationship component. But there's more. In his own words, each of the pilots explained that these two components were not enough to give a person full self-confidence. "No question, you have to have faith!" said the first, while I was questioning him further about aircraft carrier landings. "Inshallah," the second added, to describe his state of mind when the runway comes up: it's in God's hands. Technical confidence and confidence in others are not everything. They draw on a primordial source, confidence in life, which is hard to define but easy enough to feel. This confidence in life is not a confidence in something. It *is* confidence.

And this first confidence is something that, in one way or another, we all have. We don't all feel it the same way or call it by the same name, and it can vary in strength according to the kind of childhood we've had, but we all have it. Because we are alive.

To try to bring it a little more clearly into focus, let's look at this mystical dimension of self-confidence in what is perhaps its purest form: as it exists in those who have survived the worst horrors and still retain their confidence in life, and among the exceptional souls who have turned from the comforts of normal life to experience life in its most naked form.

———

Antoine Leiris lost his wife in the terrorist attack on the Bataclan theater in Paris on November 13, 2015. A few days later, he wrote a letter to his wife's assassins, which he posted on Facebook and later turned into a book, *You Will Not Have My Hate:*

> *On Friday night, you stole the life of an exceptional being, the love of my life, the mother of my son, but you will not have my hate. I don't know who you are and I don't want to know. You are dead souls. If that God for whom you blindly kill made us in his image, each bullet in my wife's body will have been a wound in his heart.*
>
> *So, no, I will not give you the satisfaction of hating you. That is what you want, but to respond to your hate with anger would be to yield to the same ignorance that made you what you are. You want me to be scared, to see my fellow citizens through suspicious eyes, to sacrifice my freedom for security. You have failed. I will not change. [. . .]*
>
> *Of course I am devastated by grief, I grant you that small victory, but it will be short-lived. I know she will be with us every day and that we will see each other in the paradise of free souls to which you will never have access.*
>
> *There are only two of us—my son and myself—but we are stronger than all the armies of the world. Anyway, I don't have any more time to waste on you, as I must go to see Melvil, who is just waking up from his nap. He is only seventeen months old. He will eat his snack as he does every day, then we will play as we do every day, and all his life this little boy will defy you by being happy and free. Because you will not have his hate either.*

This poignant letter demonstrates that even when life is unfair, when stupidity and hatred wreak a trail of destruction, we can still have faith in life. "All his life this little boy will defy you by being happy and free," says the father splendidly. This act of causing offense is how life deals with what threatens it. Of course, the war is not over. There will be difficult moments, moments of doubt and downheartedness. But that's exactly what the feeling of confidence is about. It's confidence *in spite of everything.* Having confidence in life doesn't mean thinking that life is simple and that its meaning is obvious. If that were the case, there would be no need to "have confidence" in it. A bunch of drugged and brainless fanatics murdered Antoine Leiris's wife along with 129 other people in a bloodbath at the Bataclan theater. Antoine Leiris knows that this, too, is part of his life. But when he talks about his son, who will continue to "eat his snack," to play, and grow up to be a free man, we get a taste of what confidence in life can really be. It's precisely when life is threatened that we most need to show our confidence. We have all been living this, ever since Sept. 11, 2001, ever since we entered this new age of terrorism. Our lives, our way of life, and our civilization of freedom have been attacked. Fighters have declared war on it. At any moment, a suicide bomber may blow himself up, taking innocent lives with him. One response to this troubling state of war in a time of peace is to increase our confidence in life.

In The Fire Next Time, *James Baldwin evokes* the mystery of this confidence in life that doesn't so much resist everything that might destroy it as flare out in the very presence of what threatens it:

> This past, the Negro's past, of rope, fire, torture, castra-
> tion, infanticide, rape; death and humiliation; fear by day
> and night, fear as deep as the marrow of the bone; doubt
> that he was worthy of life...rage, hatred, and murder,
> hatred for white men so deep that it often turned against
> him and his own...—this past, this endless struggle to
> achieve and reveal and confirm a human identity, human
> authority, yet contains, for all its horror, something very
> beautiful....That man who is forced each day to snatch
> his manhood, his identity, out of the fire of human cruelty
> that rages to destroy it knows, if he survives his effort, and
> even if he does not survive it, something about himself
> and human life....The apprehension of life here so briefly
> and inadequately sketched has been the experience of
> generations of Negroes, and it helps to explain how they
> have endured and how they have been able to produce
> children of kindergarten age who can walk through mobs
> to get to school.

The fact that there is "something very beautiful" in the midst of all the horrors Baldwin describes is precisely the heart of life, of this mysterious phenomenon of confidence. The child who "walks through mobs" is Ruby Bridges, the first black child to desegregate an all-white school in Louisiana in 1960. She was six years old and had to face the violence and insults of outraged racists. From her courage and determination at that young age, we can see how a confidence in life can play its part in the most immediate battles, the struggle for a more just world. With every further step taken by Ruby Bridges, we understand how right we are to have confidence in life. The most valiant political struggles often originate at this most mysterious source.

If confidence in life can paradoxically be strengthened in times of tragedy, it can also reach great heights in conditions of extreme deprivation. The great mystics have seen a glint of light in the blackest darkness.

Etty Hillesum was a young Dutch woman, born into a Jewish family in 1914, who kept an extraordinary diary: *An Interrupted Life.* She tells what happened to her between March 1941, when she was living freely in Amsterdam, and September 1943, when she was deported to Auschwitz, where she would die with her parents and brother. A cultivated, troubled woman who lived her life fully and had many lovers, often considerably older than she, Etty Hillesum was undergoing therapy in 1941 with the psychologist Julius Spier, a follower of Carl Jung, who would become her spiritual guide. It was he who urged her to seek a path toward her unusual desire. It was also he who introduced her to the Gospels and the works of both Saint Augustine and Meister Eckhart. She writes in her diary that she had the impression of being truly reborn as herself thanks to this relationship with her therapist. She also describes Spier as having led her to God. Armed with her new faith, she experienced the pure joy of living. She wanted to love and to share, to help and to embrace—sometimes to excess, as she recognizes with a touch of humor: "It is difficult to be on equally good terms with God and your body." But the roundup of Jews was increasing and becoming more intense. At first, the Nazis sent Dutch Jews to the transit camp at Westerbork, "the antechamber of the Holocaust," from which convoys regularly left for Auschwitz. Hillesum managed to escape the roundups but watched her friends, her people, being taken away. She didn't want to be left in isolation from her own kind. She applied to the Jewish council for transfer to the Westerbork camp so that she could work in the department of Social Welfare for People in Transit. She wanted to be useful to those who were suffering and bring light where there was darkness: "We should be willing to act as a balm for all wounds," she wrote. At Camp Westerbork, she felt that she had found her place. She was reunited with her parents and brother, but also united with all her many brothers and sisters who were being swept up and deported. She devoted herself to a single task in the camp hospital: making daily life a little more bearable. She set about it with joyous compassion, surprisingly lighthearted at times, deploying all her ingenuity. She gave care and reassurance, spoke out or held her tongue, brought food when she could, looked after babies when the exhausted mothers could no longer hold them. Those who survived used the same word over and over to describe her: she exuded *radiance*. Yet she quickly realized what others couldn't or wouldn't see: that the trains leaving Westerbork were on a one-way trip to death.

"I am filled with confidence," she wrote, "not that I shall succeed in worldly things, but that even when things go badly for me I shall still find life good and worth living." Reading her exceptional diaries and letters, one discovers a young woman of twenty-eight who, day after day, retained her confidence in life, in God, and in humanity, even to the brink of unnamable horror: "If there were only one human being worthy of the name of 'man,' then we should be justified in believing in men and in humanity," she wrote in her diary.

Her trust in life was not blind to the staggering evil that men were capable of. She simply accepted all of life; she consented to it: "Living and dying, sorrow and joy, the blisters on my feet and the jasmine behind the house, the persecution, the unspeakable horrors—it is all as one in me, and I accept it all as one mighty whole." In a letter dated June 8, 1943, she wrote: "The sky is full of birds, the purple lupins stand up so regally and peacefully, two little old women have sat down on the box for a chat, the sun is shining on my face—and right before our eyes, mass murder. The whole thing is simply beyond comprehension. I am well. Affectionately, Etty."

As she so accurately says, she is "well" because she accepts the incomprehensible. In this extreme situation, she maintains her confidence because she has stopped trying to understand everything. She assents to the mystery of a life that contains much evil and much good. "Of course, it is our complete destruction they want! But let us bear it with grace," she wrote a few days before leaving for Auschwitz.

We have here an example of the mystical dimension of confidence, an example of confidence in its pure state: the opposite of mastery, the inordinately heightened surrender to what is greater than oneself: "We *are* 'at home.' Under the sky. In every place on earth, if only we carry everything within us."

In every culture, and at every stage in human history, sages have renounced the immediate gratifications of life and even its most elementary comforts to renew contact with the barest form of existence. Stoic philosophers, Christian monks, Buddhists, Hindu sannyasins—they weren't torn from their comforts forcibly by any particular event. They voluntarily gave up the non-essential, the better to experience the essential and strengthen their confidence in life, without falsehood or mediation. Having stripped as much as possible of the ordinary stuff of life away, they touched life's very heart. The actions of Etty Hillesum, who went voluntarily to the Westerbork transit camp, place her within this tradition.

The example of these men and women, which is so radical it is sometimes difficult to conceive, may help us when we are dogged by bad luck or assailed by an unexpected turn of events. To still have confidence in life when we experience a setback in love or a wound to our ego is to have internalized the wisdom of the Stoic sages.

To continue to believe that life is an opportunity after meeting with defeat is to take a page from the wisdom of the Epicureans.

To love life when one has suffered the cruelty of man and the injustice of the system is to have a bit of Etty Hillesum in one's breast.

To develop an ability to bounce back and draw on creative resources when confronted with adversity is to glimpse the power of Bergson's *élan vital*.

To suddenly feel, while in the midst of being severely tested, a mad joy welling up inside, to sense that one would be able to love life even if it were to grant us nothing that we expect of it, is to make contact in the depths of oneself with this primary confidence, to draw close to the source of all the different forms of confidence.

Conclusion

I finished this book on the day French pop singer France Gall died. On the radio, her hit song "Il jouait du piano debout" (He played the piano standing up) was aired over and over:

He played the piano standing up
When cowards were on their knees
And soldiers at attention
Standing on his two feet
He wanted to be himself
You see

This song, written by Michel Berger, is a hymn to confidence. To have confidence in ourselves is to play the piano standing up, to play in a way that is recognizably our own and that lets us be free and express ourselves. It's to go forward on our two feet, with one foot in our comfort zone, the other stepping beyond it. To have confidence is to silence the coward inside us, the part of us kneeling before social norms and obstacles, and unable to say Yes to life. And to silence, too, the "soldier at attention," the part of us that finds it easier to obey orders than to listen to our own desires.

> He played the piano standing up
> That might just seem a detail to you
> But to me it meant a lot
> It meant that he was free
> Happy to be there with us

The only true freedom is the freedom to be fully oneself. We can all play the piano standing up.

This invitation to free ourselves, to listen to ourselves, repeats the opening gambit of the philosophical tradition.

Socrates does nothing if not invite his hearers to think for themselves, to have confidence in themselves. He knows one thing only, which is that he knows nothing. How can he best set his followers free? He doesn't offer them any knowledge. But he frees them from their complexes, their false opinions.

Twenty-one centuries later, Descartes proposed that, armed only with reason, we cast doubt on all that is not certain, then rebuild the edifice of knowledge on entirely new foundations.

There was never a more radical intellectual endeavor. He asks that we have absolute confidence in our reasoning.

In an echoing gesture, Pascal invited us to turn our backs on churches and priests in order to confront, alone in our study and in the secret of our heart, the truth of God. Nietzsche, on the other hand, explained that in a world without God, we must emerge from our study, climb mountains, and determine for ourselves, as Zarathustra did, the value of our lives. But it's always the same invitation to have confidence in ourselves.

We find the same exhortation in Kant, Denis Diderot, and Jean d'Alembert, who in the Age of Enlightenment would say: "Have the courage to listen to your own reason. Don't go outside yourself looking for the proper way to behave, because it can be found inside you. Have confidence in yourself. Have confidence in your critical judgment. Of course, you'll have moments of doubt. It's harder to follow your own reason than the well-worn path of prejudice. But that's how you'll raise yourself up."

The beauty of the philosophical enterprise, I believe, lies precisely in this, the invitation to self-assurance. Every philosopher sings this song in his own language and with his own concepts, most often without saying so explicitly. But all invite us to grasp our freedom, to be worthy of what makes us different, to have confidence in our star.

Every day for the past twenty years, I have taught philosophy to secondary schoolers. Nothing gives me more joy than to see them wake up, argue and criticize, wonder and debate, gain confidence in their thought, their intuition, and their future—in a word, to see them gain confidence in themselves. I tell them of philosophers who encourage confidence but at the same time sing the praises of doubt, restlessness, and a healthy wariness. They understand perfectly. They instinctively grasp what the great mystics are also telling us: if there were no doubt, there would be no need for self-confidence.

To have confidence in yourself is not to be sure of yourself. It's to have the courage to confront uncertainty rather than avoid it—to use your doubt as a push-off point and the source of your strength to go forward.

Works Contributing to This Book

INTRODUCTION

Friedrich Nietzsche, *Thus Spake Zarathustra* (1883–1885). This
    book contains the famous exhortation to "become what
    you are," a masterly invitation to self-confidence, in all its
    particularity.

Christian Bobin, Edouard Boubat, *Donne-moi quelque chose qui
    ne meure pas* (Give me something that won't die) (1996). The
    chiseled texts of Christian Bobin and the accompanying pho-
    tographs by Edouard Boubat describe how self-confidence is
    always confidence in what is beyond us.

Philip Norman, *John Lennon: The Life* (2008). This biography
    of one of the great pop stars of the twentieth century lets us

see the extent to which self-assurance is something achieved and not an innate gift.

Ralph Waldo Emerson, "Self-Reliance" (1841). This essay, by a New Englander who greatly influenced Nietzsche, is the only explicit work by a philosopher on self-confidence. A literary gem, it is also an elegy to intuition.

Henri Bergson, *Creative Evolution* (1907) and *Mind-Energy* (1919). Classics of twentieth-century philosophy, these works reveal that self-confidence can also be a faith in the creative force coursing through living beings.

Boris Cyrulnik, *Les Vilains petits canards* (Nasty little ducks) (2001) and *Les nourritures affectives* (Emotional nourishment) (1993). Neuropsychiatrist Boris Cyrulnik demonstrates that it's never too late to find or rediscover our confidence, never too late to weave or reweave the relationships that strengthen our belief in ourselves and our happiness.

Jacques Lacan, *Écrits I et II* (1966), published in English as *Écrits: The First Complete Edition in English* (2006). A difficult text by the great French psychoanalyst, but one that allows us to understand that the issue of confidence has to be considered in relation to the real, the imaginary, and the symbolic.

CHAPTER 1—CULTIVATE STRONG TIES

Aristotle, *Politics* (fourth century B.C.). One of the most important books in the history of philosophy, it posits that man is a political animal because he is incomplete. He therefore seeks to build his confidence through his relationships with others.

————, *Nicomachean Ethics* (fourth century B.C.). This work contains Aristotle's fine definition of friendship, which helps us understand our need for mentors. For the human animals that we are, confidence cannot be attained alone.

Sigmund Freud, *Five Lectures on Psychoanalysis* (1910) and *Introduction to Psychoanalysis* (1916–1917). The basic theoretical framework for understanding the theories of attachment and the need for "inner security," which derive their meaning from Freud's concept of "infantile anxiety."

Jacques Lacan, "The Mirror Stage" in *Écrits I* (1966). A short text, but it is one that is dense, fundamental, and extraordinarily powerful. It deserves to be read and reread for its exposition of the extent to which confidence is sought in the other's confirming gaze. Assurance is never simply a confidence in "self."

François Truffaut, *The Wild Child* (1970). A film classic that describes the impossibility for a child who has been severed from relationships with other humans to become fully human.

Immanuel Kant, *On Education* (1776). The great philosopher, writing at the end of the eighteenth century, explains that a good education is measured by the degree of autonomy it confers. To be well educated is to no longer need those who educated us. Self-confidence thus becomes a confidence in our own judgment, in our autonomous reason.

John Bowlby, *The Making and Breaking of Affectional Bonds* (1956–1976) and *Attachment and Loss* (1969). This British psychiatrist and psychoanalyst has written decisive works on the theory of attachment and the need for "inner security," works that were later referenced by, among others, Boris Cyrulnik.

Catherine Destivelle and Érik Decamp, *Annapurna, duo pour un 8000* (Annapurna, duet for an 8,000-meter peak) (1994). In their account of a climb, these two great mountaineers show that self-confidence is inseparable from confidence in the other. That's the lovely metaphor of a roped climbing party.

Maria Montessori, *The Secret of Childhood* (1936) and *Absorbent Mind* (1949). To understand the Montessori method, one may as well go to the source. Here, the Italian educator lays out her program, which is based on trust, encouragement, and educating the student's creativity and freedom.

James Baldwin, *The Fire Next Time* (1963). This book is significant for its power as a work of literature and its political importance. The "love" that Baldwin evokes so eloquently speaks to the importance of relational confidence. The book also testifies to the political power that has emerged from the resistance of America's black enslaved people and their descendants.

Anne Dufourmantelle, *Power of Gentleness: meditations on the risk of living* (2013). Writing in a delicate style, this French psychoanalyst argues that there is never really a lack of confidence "in oneself": it always comes down to a lack of confidence in the other.

Isabelle Filliozat, *Fais-toi confiance* (Trust yourself) (2005). This contemporary psychologist combines insightful views with a wealth of cases from her clinical practice over the past few decades.

CHAPTER 2—GO INTO TRAINING

Malcolm Gladwell, *Outliers* (2008). In this very instructive book, the *New Yorker* reporter details a fascinating investigation into how competence can turn into confidence.

Edmund Husserl, *Cartesian Meditations* (1931). In this introduction to phenomenology by one of the great philosophers of the twentieth century, we are exposed to the idea that "all consciousness is consciousness of something." Confidence, too, is first of all a confidence in oneself accomplishing something.

Heraclitus, "Fragments" (sixth century B.C.). "We do not step twice into the same river," says the pre-Socratic philosopher. Confidence can therefore not simply be mastery: it must give us the strength to deal with the unexpected.

Friedrich Nietzsche, *Thus Spake Zarathustra* (1883–1885). Worth reading for the grotesque character of the Conscientious One, the archetype of the person imprisoned by his own competence.

———, *Untimely Meditations, Part II* (1874). For its reflections on establishing a relationship with knowledge that frees us and gives us confidence, instead of walling us in.

———, *The Gay Science* (1882). For its meditations on the beneficial philosophy of "the great Yes to life."

Jean-Pierre Vernant, *Origins of Greek Thought* (1962). Valuable in particular for the way this great Hellenist characterizes the god Hephaestus: it is by doing the work of a blacksmith, not surprisingly, that a man becomes a blacksmith.

Frederick Douglass, *Narrative of the Life of Frederick Douglass, an American Slave* (1845). This book shows how a man who was meant to be turned into a beast became a free man—by training himself to read and write.

Emmanuel Delessert, *Oser faire confiance* (Daring to have confidence) (2015). In this work, the young French philosopher neatly shows us that self-confidence is not simply a question of reassurance.

CHAPTER 3—LISTEN TO YOURSELF

Immanuel Kant, *Critique of Judgment* (1790). In this third critique, which followed the *Critique of Pure Reason* (1781) and the *Critique of Practical Reason* (1788), the German philosopher defines the beautiful as "the free and harmonious play of the human faculties." The aesthetic experience is a moment of inner attunement. There is no true self-confidence without a capacity to listen to oneself.

————, "An Answer to the Question: What Is Enlightenment?" (1784). In this short text, Kant posits that enlightenment is the capacity to "have the courage to make use of one's own understanding." To trust oneself is to have confidence in one's own thought.

Ralph Waldo Emerson, *Essays* (1841). These essays include "Self-Reliance" and "Nature." Listening to oneself is learning to listen to one's intuition, "that gleam of light that flashes across [one's] mind from within."

Antoine de Saint-Exupéry, *The Little Prince* (1943). We find here, articulated by Saint-Exupéry's fox, a succinct argument in favor of rites and rituals. Without them, how would we manage to listen to ourselves?

Henri Bergson, *The Creative Mind: An Introduction to Metaphysics* (1934). This collection, one of whose texts addresses intuition, provides the best possible entry into Bergson's philosophy.

Friedrich Nietzsche, *Writings from the Late Notebooks* (1901) Here, Nietzsche speaks of his admiration for the author of "Self-Reliance": "Emerson. Never have I felt so much at home in a book, and in my *own* home—I may not praise it, it is too close to me."

Fabrice Midal, *Comprendre l'art moderne* (Understanding modern art) (2010). The philosopher and meditation instructor shows us in detail, and by using specific works of art as examples, that learning to look at the artworks of the twentieth century is learning to listen to oneself.

CHAPTER 4—EXPOSE YOURSELF TO WONDER

Charles Baudelaire, *Curiosités esthétiques* (1868), in *Selected Writings on Art and Literature*. In these texts, the poet supports his statement that "the beautiful is always bizarre." Strange indeed is the power that beauty gives us: it authorizes us to finally listen to and trust ourselves.

Immanuel Kant, *Critique of Judgment* (1790). This classic of philosophy is relevant to us here because it treats the question of how, strangely enough, the harmony in external nature creates harmony within our subjective selves, quiets interior conflict, and gives us confidence in our free judgment.

Henry David Thoreau, *Walden; or, Life in the Woods* (1854). In this masterpiece, a deep reflection on the bond between man and nature, Emerson's friend Thoreau tells of living in a cabin by a pond in Massachusetts. It helps us understand why a walk in nature allows us to regain our confidence.

Jean-Paul Janssen, *La vie au bout des doigts* (Life at one's fingertips) (1982). This short documentary film featuring the climber Patrick Edlinger offers a perfect illustration of how natural beauty can play into self-confidence.

Marcus Aurelius, *Meditations* (second century B.C.). An emperor and a Stoic philosopher, Marcus Aurelius speaks of the cosmic energy that maintains the world in balance. How can we not have confidence in life when we live in the midst of such harmony?

Victor Hugo, *Les Chansons des rues et des bois* (Songs of street and wood) (1865). In the poem "Nature is full of love," Hugo depicts nature as brimming with enough life to carry us and give us confidence.

Henri Bergson, *Creative Evolution* (1907). In this work, Bergson develops his notion of *élan vital*, or vital impetus, a creative spontaneity that accounts for the evolution of living beings and that courses through us when we are inventive, free, and confident.

François Cheng, *The Way of Beauty: Five Meditations for Spiritual Transformation* (2006). This book of meditations is a sustained reflection on the powers of beauty: "Beauty is something that is present virtually, that has always been present, a desire bubbling up from within individual beings, or from Being itself, like an inexhaustible fountain."

François Jullien, *The Strange Idea of the Beautiful* (2010). The philosopher and China expert shows how beauty can make us present to the world: "The beautiful is there, like a glacial erratic in a changed world, like a holdover from the time of the gods."

Charles Pépin, *Quand la beauté nous sauve* (When beauty saves us) (2013). I published this book a few years ago and could easily have called it "When beauty saves us from a crisis of confidence." The ideas in the present chapter amplify the thoughts developed in the earlier book.

CHAPTER 5—DECIDE

Seneca, *Letters to Lucilius* (first century A.D.). In this masterpiece, consisting of 124 letters by the great Stoic philosopher, we find all the major themes of Stoic thinking, including what amounts to a defense of decision-making: "Accidents happen hour after hour that require a decision, and it's to philosophy that one must turn." Having self-confidence is learning to make decisions.

Blaise Pascal, *Pensées* (1670). "God is not a question of proof but of experience," wrote this Christian apologist. From which we can understand just how much self-confidence has also to be confidence in something more than ourselves.

Søren Kierkegaard, "Diary of a Seducer," from *Either/Or* (1843); *Fear and Trembling* (1843); *Concluding Unscientific Postscript* (1846). In all these major works by the Danish existentialist philosopher, faith appears as a "leap" beyond reason, a pure decision, and not a rational choice. It takes a full measure of self-confidence to decide in the face of uncertainty, to trust oneself in the midst of doubt.

Jean-Paul Sartre, *Existentialism and Humanism* (1946). This is a short lecture that clearly exposes the link between trusting our freedom and being able to make decisions. To an existentialist, self-confidence is above all confidence in our own freedom.

————, *Being and Nothingness* (1943). This is a long and difficult text, which argues that the anxiety provoked by the need for action is nothing other than "the reflexive seizure of freedom by its own self," in other words, a sign of our freedom. The decision to act allows us to emerge from this anguish and take stock of the extent of our freedom.

CHAPTER 6—GET YOUR HANDS DIRTY

Matthew B. Crawford, *Shop Class as Soulcraft: An Inquiry into the Value of Work* (2009). Here is an astonishing book, combining theory and life history, by an author with a Ph.D. in philosophy who explains how he found self-confidence by becoming a motorcycle mechanic.

Aristotle, *Nicomachean Ethics* (fourth century B.C.). Each person, says Aristotle, should have work that allows him to achieve his own perfection and therefore have confidence in himself.

————, *On the Parts of Animals* (fourth century B.C.). This is the work in which Aristotle argues that the hand is an extension of human intelligence. By doing nothing with our hands, we risk being cut off from a part of ourselves.

Karl Marx, *Economic and Philosophic Manuscripts of 1844*. Marx criticizes work in a capitalist economy, but not work per se. In fact, he has written a number of beautiful passages on the ideal conditions for work, where it would be neither exploitation nor alienation but an opportunity for self-realization, for developing one's personality, for self-confidence.

G. W. F. Hegel, *Phenomenology of Mind* (1807). In his dialectic of "the master and the slave," Hegel shows how much we need gratitude and recognition, as well as true contact with the things of this world, in order to gain confidence in ourselves, realize our value, and construct our happiness.

Henri Bergson, *Creative Evolution* (1907). Bergson defines humans in this text more as *Homo faber* than as *Homo sapiens*: "Intelligence, conceived in what appears to be its original capacity, is the faculty of making artifacts, especially tools for making other tools, and to vary the manufacture indefinitely." If our deep nature is to be *Homo faber*, we understand how our confidence can suffer when we "make" nothing: we then need to reestablish ourselves as "makers" to regain confidence.

Michel Serres, *Pantopie, de Hermès à Petite Poucette, entretiens avec Martin Legros et Sven Ortoli* (Pantopia, from Hermes to Thumbelina, discussions with Martin Legros and Sven

Ortoli) (2014). The author discusses the disappearance of the rural way of life and all that has been carried away with it.

Georges Charpak, ed., *La Main à la pâte, les sciences à l'école primaire* (Hands-on: science at the primary school level) (2011). In this book, the Nobel Prize–winning physicist describes ingenious and concrete experiments (establishing the boiling point of water, understanding the principle of buoyancy, seeing the air we breathe, making an hourglass...) that allow children not only to discover science but also to develop their personalities and have confidence in themselves.

CHAPTER 7—SWING INTO ACTION

Alain, *Alain on Happiness* (1925). The author provides a true philosophy of action: action is not secondary to thought but has its own distinct value, its truth.

G. W. F. Hegel, *Phenomenology of Mind* (1807). Even the Mind needs to act in order to know itself, even God must come to action to know his own value. The same thing is true for us: we must not wait to act until we are completely sure of ourselves but act in order to gain confidence along the way.

Marcus Aurelius, *Meditations* (second century A.D.). A belief in fate, we learn here, doesn't rule out the need for a defense of action. To act is not to think that everything depends on us, but to act on all that does depend on us, while readily accepting all that doesn't. Self-confidence is not arrogance. It is at the same time humility and a broadened confidence: humility because everything doesn't depend on us; and broadened confidence because by acting we show confidence in what doesn't depend on us, but which our action may set in motion.

Jean-Paul Sartre, *Transcendence of the Ego: An Existentialist Theory of Consciousness* (1936). Our "me," or ego, has value not in and of itself but outside itself, in the world that it subdues through its actions, and in the relationships it thereby creates with others. One must come out of oneself, out of one's comfort zone, in order to have self-confidence.

CHAPTER 8—ADMIRE

Sigmund Freud, *Civilization and Its Discontents* (1930). In this short, masterful text, Freud shows that what is good for society (the norm) is not good for the individual (the expression of his singularity). Hence the "discontent." How are we to have confidence in our singularity in a society that values the norm? By admiring others, as Nietzsche tells us, who have developed their singularity and have dared to become themselves despite the pressure of social norms.

Michel Crépu, *L'Admiration. Contre l'idolâtrie* (Admiration; against idolatry) (2017). Idolatry diminishes the idolater, while admiration heightens the admirer, as we learn from this contemporary essay by an erudite literary critic.

CHAPTER 9—STAY TRUE TO YOUR DESIRE

Baruch Spinoza, *Ethics* (1677). Spinoza defines joy as "the passage from a lesser to a greater perfection." The joy of progressing, of developing, protects us from the temptation to compare ourselves to others, which is poison to our self-confidence.

Anthony Storr, *Solitude* (1988). A lovely essay, in which this Jungian psychoanalyst argues for the benefits of solitude—not isolation—in building one's individuality, listening to one's desire, and developing one's imagination and creativity. We are all of us alone in being what we are—we are all of us solitaire diamonds. We have to know this to have self-confidence.

Jacques Lacan, *Ethics of Psychoanalysis* (1986). In this essay, Jacques Lacan delves into the idea of being faithful to one's desire. All of us have *desires*. But our *own* desire is what we need to have faith in. This is our unconscious axis, our "affair," as Lacan calls it, our secret coherence. When we are unfaithful to it, we are cut off from ourselves, and our sense of guilt keeps us from having self-confidence, sometimes leading us into depression. Self-confidence is keeping faith with oneself, with one's desire or quest.

Homer, *Odyssey* (eighth century B.C.). An attentive reading of this classic shows us that Ulysses represents the hero who is armed with self-knowledge and who is faithful to his desire despite the temptations and enchantments put in his way. Ulysses derives self-confidence from knowing his true desire.

CHAPTER 10—TRUST THE MYSTERY

Lucretius, *On the Nature of Things* (first century B.C.). This sublime poem awakens us to the mystery of the random nature of the world and the miracle of our existence. Having self-confidence starts with the consciousness of our great luck in having emerged from nothingness to exist at all.

Henri Bergson, *Mind-Energy* (1919). In this book, probably Bergson's most important, the philosopher defines life as the *élan vital*, the mysterious spiritual force at the heart of matter. Self-confidence is confidence in the creativity that fills us when we allow it to, notably when we turn away from repetition and habit.

Edmund Husserl, *Ideas: General Introduction to Pure Phenomenology* (1913). In this late work, Husserl develops the lovely idea of an "original confidence" in the world. To be born is to be entrusted to the world and to have a corresponding original confidence in it. Self-confidence is based on this primal confidence in the world around us.

Maurice Merleau-Ponty, *The Visible and the Invisible* (1964) and *Phenomenology of Perception* (1945). Like Husserl, this French phenomenologist believes that we are of this world and caught up in its "fabric," its "flesh." There can be no self-confidence without the sense of living in the world and being at home in the world.

Christian Bobin, *L'épuisement* (Exhaustion) (2015) and *Les ruines du ciel* (Heaven's ruins) (2009). A mystical Christian, Bobin is an inspired prose writer who finds beauty in the simplest aspects of daily life. For him, self-confidence is confidence in this life, whose every microfragment has been illuminated by the brief passage of Christ on earth. He believes, as Emerson does, that self-trust begins with a trust in something larger than oneself.

Pascal Quignard, *Vie secrète* (Secret life) (1997). In this wonderful novel, Quignard (who is also a poet and essayist and whose *Roving Shadows* won the Prix Goncourt in 2002) writes the following: "Defeat comes from inside oneself. There is no defeat in the outside world. Nature, the sky, night, rain, and wind are a long, unseeing triumph"—the triumph of a life as mysterious in its existence as in its perseverance. Having confidence in oneself is keeping oneself as close as possible to this mystery, this triumph.

Antoine Leiris, *You Will Not Have My Hate* (2016). In this account, written by a man who lost his wife in the Bataclan massacre in Paris on Nov. 13, 2015, and was left to raise the couple's son on his own, confidence in life opposes death, injustice, and hatred. It even seems to offer an answer to them.

Etty Hillesum, *An Interrupted Life* (1985). This diary of a young Dutch woman deported to Auschwitz where she was killed in 1943 is a masterpiece. She displays a confidence in life that doesn't quit, even in the concentration camps. From the fact of being alive, we all have in us just such a confidence in life, in one form or another. It nourishes our self-confidence.

Index

CHARLES PÉPIN is a philosopher and novelist whose work has been published in some thirty countries. He is the author of *Philosophers on the Couch*, *When Beauty Saves Us*, and *Joy*. His latest essay, *The Virtues of Failure*, has sold more than 65,000 copies and been translated and published in thirteen countries. With the designer Jul, Charles published the best sellers *The Planet of the Wise* and *50 Shades of Greeks*. He is also the organizer of the Lundis Philo lecture series at MK2 Odéon in Paris.

WILLARD WOOD is the winner of the 2002 Lewis Galantière Award for Literary Translation and a 2000 National Endowment for the Arts Fellowship in Translation. He lives in Connecticut.